Home Renovations

THE COMPLETE HANDBOOK

Paul Hymers

NEW HOLLAND

First published in 2004 by New Holland Publishers (UK) Ltd
Garfield House, 86–88 Edgware Road
London W2 2EA
United Kingdom
London • Cape Town • Sydney • Auckland
www.newhollandpublishers.com

ISBN 1 84330 696 4

Senior Editor: Clare Sayer
Editor: Ian Kearey
Designer: Casebourne Rose Design Associates
Illustrator: Sue Rose
Cover photograph: Hannah Mornement

Printed and bound by Kyodo Printing Co (Singapore) Pte Ltd

DECLARATION

Acknowledgements
Thanks as always to my friends and colleagues for sharing with me their knowledge
and experience, and in particular to Conservation Officers Clive and Sarah.
Thanks also to my decorating brothers-in-law Mark and Nick (M&G Decorators) and
other assorted trades- and craftsmen.

Page 17 – image reproduced from Ordnance Survey map.

Contents

Introduction

ENOVATING homes is one of the UK's most popular pastimes, and it's not difficult to see why – we are fortunate to have a wealth of history in our buildings. But renovating isn't just for those who own a period home; it is for anyone who wants to improve their place for today and for tomorrow. For many home-owners, even redecorating is so much more than painting the walls: it can mean stripping doors or fitting creative lighting, laying hardwood flooring or redesigning the bathroom. Engulfed by ideas of interior design and architecture, we are always looking to improve our living space, and there is so much scope to do this in older properties.

Our newly built homes are becoming smaller and more tightly packed together than ever before. Since 1980 the average size of a new home has dropped by 5 sq m to 83 sq m. Those third and fourth bedrooms in 'family homes' have become incredibly small in

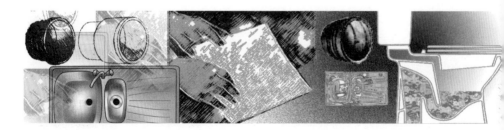

recent years, and most often need a purpose-made bed to be useable. Even in Victorian homes the cot room was never this small, so one attraction of older homes is obvious – space.

Space not just inside but out, where you can open the front door without having to rub shoulders with the neighbouring house and onto a garden that isn't bordered by six other homes, all overlooking it. Older homes have bigger rooms, better features and longer gardens, but only when they are renovated do we really appreciate them.

Renovation work doesn't have to be major before it becomes worthwhile; smaller projects, like refitting the kitchen or refurbishing a fireplace, go a long way to transforming a home, and are just as rewarding. Whether you're restoring a period cottage, replacing the windows in a 1970s semi or improving the insulation in a bungalow, *Home Renovations* is the front door key to a better home. Don't leave it under a brick!

CHAPTER ONE

Preliminaries

Empty homes

In 2003 England was recorded as having 21.1 million homes, which was 800,000 up on the last count in 1996. We tend to add about 150,000 new ones every year to the grand total, and to do this, many of them are built on green land – the countryside. Very soon we are going to have to find a way to slow that down. Brownfield sites offer some potential for redevelopment as new homes, but more promise lies in empty buildings waiting to be renovated.

The statistics for the same year reveal that some 300,000 dwellings stood empty and unused, and if you add to this vacant commercial buildings, the total was nearer 700,000 – a few years' worth of not building over the countryside. And these, you understand, are the long-term empty, which have become a nuisance. Some local authorities have started to compile lists of long-term unoccupied homes and are developing strategies for dealing with them. Many fall into disrepair and attract complaints of damp and vermin, or become dangerous, with loose roof tiles and broken windows. Empty homes aren't popular, make the neighbourhood look unpleasant and can bring down the value of adjoining homes.

These dwellings are owned by somebody, but it is often somebody who has no means to improve them or desire to sell them, perhaps because there is no incentive to do either. If grants or VAT relief were available, combined with free advice and equity release from mortgage lenders, many of these places could be renovated back into homes. If any further incentive is needed, homes that have been unoccupied for too long can lose their residential status in planning terms or risk compulsory purchase or enforced sale.

The joy of renovating

Let's be brave about this and face up to the truth for a moment. Building work is unpopular. It's unsightly, messy, noisy, inconvenient and stressful, and everybody, including the people engaged in it, at some time becomes unhappy with it. Nothing will change that. The best you can do is to try to minimise each of those characteristics to the point where building work is tolerable, safe in the knowledge that it won't last forever and that in the end your home will be a much better place for it.

In the case of renovation work, that 'end result' is all the more tangible. Buildings that are neglected become unpopular by themselves; it just takes a lot longer because people become used to them looking derelict and fail to notice them until they begin to collapse. In Building Control we call this phenomenon the 'Five o'clock Friday' syndrome, because more dangerous structures are reported at this time than on any other by concerned members of the public. It isn't that at this hour and on this day of the week a building that has been derelict for years suddenly and inexplicably becomes dangerous, it is because people have begun to notice it, and the nagging feeling that they should tell somebody about it becomes irrepressible once they know that there will be nobody in an office to tell for a couple of days.

Renovation work has one added advantage over all other building projects – that of being able to restore something to its former glory; to bring it back from the brink and make it look good again. People like buildings that look good, and the end result of proper renovation is always a positive one. I'll give you an example – a terraced home occupied by an alcoholic, which had become derelict to the point where the external soil pipe had broken and was left to discharge over the garden. Not a nice place for neighbours. The house was bought by a developer; his plans to extend and renovate were enthusiastically objected to by the neighbours, yet after a few months of building work the property was restored to being a quality family home, and joining the line of those interested in buying it were, you've guessed it, some of the neighbours. It helps, of course, if work progresses relatively quickly – most property developers want to do this and get the place sold before they have to pay too many instalments on their loans.

Home condition

Most of us don't wait that long before carrying out home improvements. In changing and improving our living space, we are maintaining our buildings for the future all the time.

You may already know what renovation work to do, but if you're looking at your home for the first time, it will help to survey it from top to bottom.

If you have the opportunity to spend an hour or two in any home, you can learn a significant amount about its condition by looking and taking notes. Home-condition reports may well be mandatory with every property conveyance one day, but assessing the condition of your present home or a potential purchase will help you to decide what renovations are needed.

The checklist below could be used as a pro forma for completion on a walk-through inspection. It isn't intended to replace a professional survey, which will, in the case of a 'structural survey', take longer and require and some element of minor disturbance (raised floorboards, etc), but it will help you to get a picture of the home's condition.

Date of inspection
Address of property
Date property was built
Listed or in a Conservation Area
Flats – which floor and how many in block
Tenure

ROOMS (size)	Reception	Bedrooms	Bathroom/ shower	Kitchen	Utility	Study	Other rooms
Basement							
Lower GF							
Ground floor							
First floor							
Second floor							
Total number							

DESCRIPTION AND CONDITION OF CONSTRUCTION – EXTERNAL

Roof	
Roof covering	
Chimney stack	
Rainwater gutters	
Fascias and soffits	
Walls	
Insulation	
Claddings	
Windows and doors	
Floors	
Solid or suspended	
Sub-floor ventilation	

If system built	YES/NO	type of system	
Services connected or available for connection			

Drainage foul		Mains or tank	
Drainage rainwater		Mains or soakaway	
Gas		Electricity	

Water	

Garage	YES/NO	Size	

Notes on position and condition of garage

DESCRIPTION AND CONDITION OF CONSTRUCTION – INTERNAL

. Attic	
Damp	
Ceilings	
Internal walls and partitions	
Floor finishings	
Fireplaces, flues and chimneys	
Internal woodwork	
Kitchen fittings	
Bathroom fittings	
Internal decoration	
Basements	

SERVICE INSTALLATION

Electricity	
Cooking	
Heating	
Power points	
Lighting	
Certificates of test or installation	
Gas	
Cooking	
Heating/hot water	
Water	
Metered	
Loft tanks (plastic/asbestos)	

Heating	
Vented system	
Unvented system	
Boiler	
Fuel	
Flue type	
Age	
Controls	

Garden	
Boundary	
Walls	
Fences	
Hedges	
Outbuildings	

ISSUES TO BE INVESTIGATED DURING CONVEYANCING

Tick if applicable

❏ Rights of way

❏ Covenants

❏ Adopted or private road

❏ Easements

❏ Planning Permissions granted and refused

❏ Building Regulation Approvals and Completion Certificates

❏ Environmental issues: flooding, mining, subsidence risk, etc.

Inspecting and recording

I've done it myself, so don't think I'm winding you up, but getting outside your home when it's pouring with rain is the way to find out what defects it has. Viewing it over a cold glass of beer on a hot summer's day from a reclining position behind sunglasses is less useful, even if your inspection will take much longer and seem almost mesmeric to an onlooker.

In heavy rain you see if your gutters are working, or whether they are leaking from the joints or spilling water over the top, whether your valley gutters and lead flashings are discharging the water, and whether the tiles are even and level.

It's also worth visiting your loft when it's raining to see if any water is dripping through. On very cold and windy days lofts also tell you if the pipework and water tanks are properly lagged; you'll see the steam rising from the hot water system if

they aren't, and water vapour will be condensing on the underside of the roofing felt if there isn't enough cross-ventilation in the roof void.

When inspecting your home, it is always best to start from the roof and work down one floor and one room at a time. Use a palette knife to slide between the joints of timber beams and joists, and a penknife to probe timber for soundness. Look for powdery or dark-stained timber, cracked and crazed paint or woodwork with a deteriorating paint finish – all these need to be inspected closely.

In period homes, some of the defects you find may be historic and of no consequence, while others may be more recent. Look out for physical changes to the walls, where doors or windows have been removed and the openings have been bricked up. Mortar that doesn't match is an indication of repairs or previous openings infilled.

Comparing your home with neighbouring properties can be a useful way of identifying what alterations have been made to it. Compare the design of the windows, the shape of the roof and the roof covering, but also look for unique details in the walls. At times when I've been uncertain how a roof structure has been altered to its present condition, a friendly neighbour has allowed access to their unaltered loft for me to compare the two.

Recording everything helps you prioritise your work and draft a renovation plan later. List the items of work individually and award them a priority rating and a trade; the priority rating will be based on what additional damage will be caused by not attending to the problem.

You could also include a reference to which trade would be needed for each piece of work, and this can help to group work together.

PRIORITY TABLE

1 Urgent – immediate action required for safety reasons

2 Essential – action needed soon to avoid further damage or compromise safety

3 Desirable – action beneficial to maintain or improve home, and for home efficiency and property value

4 Optional – action only needed if work is cost-effective (i.e. it can be incorporated with other work of higher priority)

Troubleshooting
Roof coverings

Roof coverings need to be renovated from time to time, and if they haven't been renovated for too long, they need to be replaced. More often than not, some tiles or slates can be salvaged and re-used, but to assess the condition from the ground, look for:

● Cracks and splits

● Slippage

● Delamination

● Colour change

● Missing slates or tiles

● Moss and vegetation growth

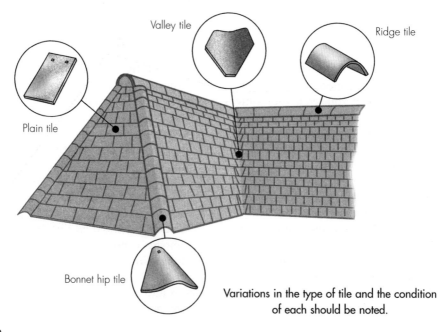

Valley tile

Ridge tile

Plain tile

Bonnet hip tile

Variations in the type of tile and the condition of each should be noted.

● Mortar missing from ridges, hips and verges.

Moss may look pretty on an old cottage roof, but it can attract damp and lead to slates splitting. You can use fungicidal washes to clean off your roof coverings, but don't be tempted to spray on acrylic-based paint finishes afterwards to 'protect' them.

Matching materials is essential, but this isn't possible for every single roof. Some tiles fade in colour so much over the years that they are unrecognisable alongside their new replacements. In such a situation you may want to consider replacing all the tiles on one slope at least, to maintain an acceptable appearance.

Delamination is the common process of decay for many slates: ultimately the layers erode away to leave a slate too thin to resist the weather. Natural slate is prone to this, but it takes a century or more to occur; asbestos slates tend to decompose in a similar way, covering your loft with black dust if no roofing felt exists to catch it. It is essential that asbestos slates are removed by approved contractors wearing protective clothing and masks; the slates need to be bagged whole, and not dropped to the ground to be swept up later. They also have to be disposed of at a registered waste disposal site for asbestos material.

Thatch can become holed or grooved to reveal its fixings, or it may start to decay and allow vegetation to grow on it. It is possible to repair thatch or overlay it without having to recover the whole roof, but you need to use local materials to match in and a skilled craftsmen to do the job. Roofs can be covered with galvanised wire netting to stop birds and squirrels from raiding it for nest material. Thatched roofs are warm roofs, and the attic should be kept draught-free with a large enough trap door to give access for fire fighting. Inspections on chimney flues and electrical circuits are essential to reduce the risk of fire in homes with thatched roofs.

Roof structures

Don't attempt to straighten up crooked or deflected roofs in historic properties – you may cause more damage by breaking joints and the like. Homes built since the late 19th century that have been retiled in more recent years may suffer now with deflecting rafters if these weren't strengthened at the time. You may need to arrest the deflection with suitable struts and purlins to prevent further sagging, rather than attempting to prop up the rafters, but this will depend on how long the roof has been suffering from the extra weight.

Chimney stacks

Leaning chimneys may need to be restrained with tie rods to stop them moving any further, but the cause of the lean should also be investigated. The chimney may have been built too slender and is now suffering under wind loads, or the mortar joint may have been weakened by sulphurous gas from the flue. If it is too badly damaged, it should be taken down and rebuilt.

External walls

- Cleaning brickwork needs careful consideration: a hundred years of ageing can be lost in one day by restoring the colour of the bricks. If it doesn't look right against other neighbouring buildings, you won't be able to put it right for another century or more.

- Even cleaning walls or stripping paint from brickwork can require Listed Building Consent.

- Individual bricks that have spalled or cracked can be cut and replaced, but if you can't find a suitable match you may be able to turn the brick around, taking care not to damage it in the process.

- Stonework repairs can be done by piecing in sourced stones, or, if this isn't possible, by using artificial or plastic repair materials that contain lime-based mortars.

- Rendered walls can suffer from bulging in places where the key to the wall behind has been lost. By tapping the wall you can hear whether it is sound or hollow behind. Loose render can be hacked off, and you can re-render to match.

Timber-frame walls

Five common ailments to look for are:

- Dry and wet rot

- Mould

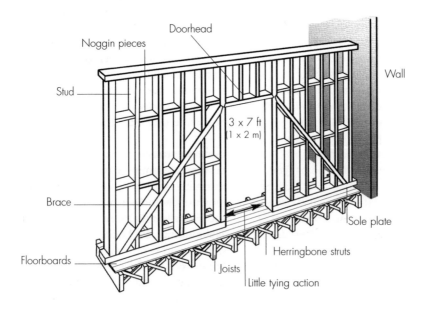

A traditional timber frame partition structure.

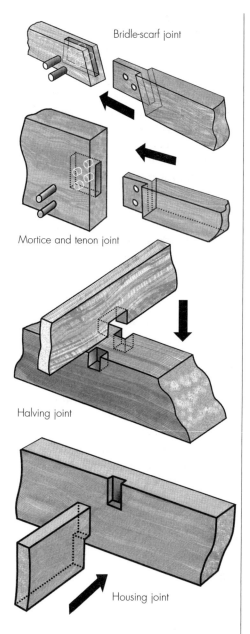

Bridle-scarf joint

Mortice and tenon joint

Halving joint

Housing joint

Traditional forms of timber joints

- Insect attack (laths are prone to beetle attack)

- Splits and shakes

- Distortion

Remember that distortion of old timber is often a characteristic feature, and not a structural failure. Green timber may have been used in the construction because it was more workable, and may have undergone a drawn-out drying process over time. Traditional timber-framed walls had diagonal braces between the studs to stiffen them, but if they've been cut through to form an opening or have suffered deterioration, they may need to be replaced.

Before the advent of plasterboard in the 1950s, plaster was keyed to walls on timber laths, an ancient technique that predates plaster and is known as wattle and daub. Woven oak staves and hazel withies formed the laths, which were then coated with sand, clay, manure or cow dung, mixed with straw or hair for reinforcement. You may be reluctant to renovate an historic wall using these materials, and lime plaster on new laths may be an acceptable alternative; ask for guidance from your local authority Conservation Officer and other bodies listed in the Contacts at the end of the book.

Dating your home

Knowing the date of your home, or at least the decade in which it was built, is for many people only momentarily interesting, but when you're renovating a home, knowing its date of birth or even the era from which it originates is a definite bonus. It may give you a clue as to how it was constructed and what materials were used – for example, homes built in the late 1940s, when building materials were hard to come by, have been known to be 'materially lean': I've even found notes in bottles built into the walls by the builders, apologising for the secondhand or poor materials used. 1960s homes may have pitch fibre drains and early trussed-rafter roofs, and so on.

Knowing your home's date will also help you to restore original period features or have some appreciation for the style of its architecture. Whether you choose to restore it in the original style is neither here nor there – if you understand how old your home is and how it was constructed, any renovation work you propose can be done with your eyes open from a position of understanding, if not actual empathy.

There are only three ways to date any building accurately, by which I mean to the year: personal knowledge, documentary evidence and signs.

Personal knowledge

This doesn't take a lot of explaining, but it either exists or it doesn't. I know that my home was built from late 1984 through to June 1985 because I was there at the time. The knowledge needn't be first-hand, and can be divulged by somebody else, a local person who has lived nearby, or their friends and relatives, may know some of the home's history. I think this is the best kind of knowledge, and it's invaluable to new home-owners.

I recently met a self-build developer who had been visited by some people in their nineties who had lived and worked on the redeveloped site in the first half of the last century. They were able to tell him where the old cesspool was and how it had been covered over, and many other useful details that were otherwise unrecorded. Of course personal knowledge has a life expectancy, and when it's gone, it's gone, so if you are lucky enough to capture some of it, record it for the future.

Documentary evidence

This takes research and a bit of time to uncover, but it is surprising how much historical information can be found on properties. You can start by viewing old maps of the area, since large-scale Ordnance Survey sheets are scaled sufficiently big to show individual properties, whether they be terraced town houses or detached farms. The first OS maps were prepared in 1872, but prior to this maps tend to be less detailed on a smaller scale. Some antique maps can be found on Internet websites that allow you to view the extract on screen, but you cannot print it without paying a fee.

The most obvious source of documentary evidence comes from the deeds of the property, and if you didn't receive them with exchange of contracts, your only other hope lies with the Land Registry Office. Regionally based, the Land Registry is the font of all knowledge when it

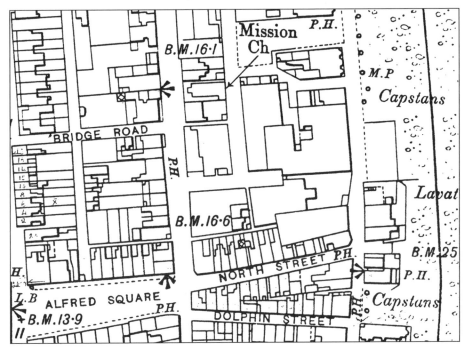

Old OS maps can be useful sources of information about a site.

comes to who owned a property and when, but is amazingly ignorant over any other issue regarding a home. If the deeds don't specify where the boundary is, the Land Registry can't help you. They can send you a copy of the registered title to the home indicating past and present ownership, and sometimes an OS extract with a thick red pen line around the boundary, but that's about it.

The deeds to older homes may be available still in their original form (they might be hand-drawn in ink on parchment) and set out the extent of the home and its land, together with the sum of the sale and parties involved. It may not help you with the actual date of construction, but it does a useful job of giving you border lines from which you can work backwards.

We have been experiencing a home-building boom in parts of the UK since the late-1990s, but not for the first time: 1890–1910 saw 20 years of mass home-building, and the next boom was in the 1950s and 1960s. Twenty-year periods of frenzied construction seem to be all we can sustain before going bust again and waiting for the next boom. When you're trying to date a property it helps to know when these boom and bust periods were; if nothing else, this reduces the odds of getting the date wrong.

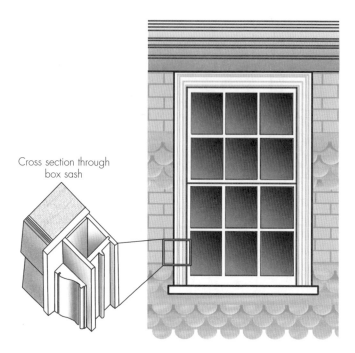

Cross section through box sash

Typical boxed sash window.

Properties from the last century may have records held with service companies - electricity, water, etc.

Signs

These are my favourite dating methods. A brick or a wall stone with the date embossed on it takes a lot of the hard work out of dating. The Edwardians were very keen on putting dates on buildings, and as many as 90 per cent have dates somewhere. If a date isn't on your home, it could be on another in the terrace.

Dates are often located on the front elevation, but sometimes they can be a little harder to find: a date carved in Roman numerals on a primary timber beam or post, or even a newspaper beneath the floorboards or a message in a bottle. They are always invaluable, and I encourage everyone to record the date of any new or renovation work on their home in some way or another.

Dating by architecture and materials

If you are still reading this section, I assume you have drawn a blank on all of the methods above and are faced with the daunting prospect of having to date your home by its architecture and materials. This isn't easy, largely because we have a tendency as a nation to try to mimic past styles, which is not a tendency confined to modern times: the Victorians were

With extensions and alterations over the years, the architecture of homes can vary. Dating parts of it rather than the whole building becomes necessary.

very fond of retro-architecture and often revived past styles.

The materials your home is built from can help because we know when they were first introduced to the country or manufactured here, and you can set dates as border lines in the past from which to work forward. Bricks, for example, were first introduced to house building in 1480, but these were imported and were not indigenous to Britain until much later. In the 1850s our own home-grown brick industry took off (the first Fletton bricks appeared in 1889), and Dutch bricks had been very popular before then.

Throughout this book I have referred to dates and times in which various features prevailed or originated, but something roughly in date order might prove useful. Below, therefore, is an abridged version of a short history of house architecture in Britain, pocket-sized and ready to be challenged by the experts.

15th century
No glass in windows yet, as they were simply openings in walls with bars or

English classicism in window proportions.

shutters on to keep the weather and the uninvited out. Bricks were first used in this century.

16th century

Coal was first used in fires between 1530 and 1540; before that wood was burned. In the late 16th century fireplaces with chimneys arrived and meant one thing – putting your hearth on an outside wall, rather than in the middle. Before then it had been the style in Great Halls to have the hearth in the middle, which was largely achievable by the fact that there were no upper floors. When people did get around to adding floors, the first thing that had to be moved was the central hearth and chimney.

Other features of the Tudor period were stepped gable walls, which formed terraces as they went up, and the use of central arches. The Tudors were also fond of using the diamond or diaper pattern in their brickwork, formed from burnt headers.

Tile fillet up the inside of a Dutch gable

Dutch gable.

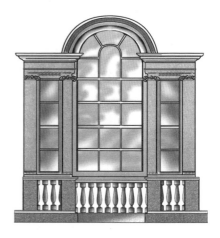

A grand Venetian window in the classical Palladian style (circa 1650–1750).

17th century

Compass gable end walls were the in style of 1670, and were so-called because they were set out by a compass. They took the Tudor stepped gable one step further with a symmetrical rounded apex. Dutch bricks were used and these are instantly recognisable by their size: at 50 mm they are much smaller than later English bricks.

Sash windows were first introduced in 1618, with the style being six panes over six panes. The fenestration arrangement of the glass panes in sash windows can tell you a lot about the age of the house – apparently, the more panes you had in a window, the more important the room was. Servants' rooms in the lower part of the house therefore had fewer windows, and the entrance levels with their reception rooms the most, in a 'Look how wealthy we are' statement. You will be hard-pushed to find many

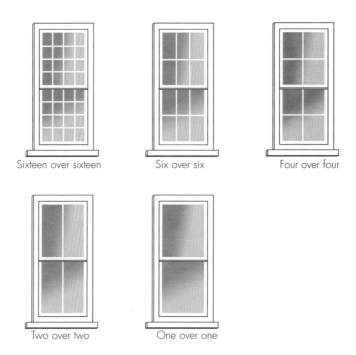

Sixteen over sixteen   Six over six   Four over four

Two over two   One over one

The evolution of sash fenestration to larger panes.

timber-framed buildings in the centre of London built before 1666, for the very obvious reason that a fair bit of the city's housing stock (13,000 homes) was lost that year to fire.

18th century
The Queen Anne period (1702–14) is notable by raised brick or stone quoins on the corners of walls, some of which were painted, and by arched windows that were arcaded (recessed) into the wall's external surface.

The first Building Act of 1707 introduced fire-break requirements separating homes in London. Party walls had to go up through the roof to form a fire barrier, and the windows had to be set back at least 100 mm

from the wall. Although the Act only applied to London, other parts of the country soon adopted the same standard, and terraces of homes soon appeared with brick party walls erupting from the roof. From 1709 windows had to be set back into the wall with a rebate in the frame, so rebated window frames don't occur before this time.

Later Georgian and Regency styles were for stone- and stucco-faced buildings, particularly during George III's reign, because apparently he hated bricks, so many brick walls were covered by render known as stucco.

Georgian architecture is mostly renowned for its windows, which became bigger; to keep the six-over-six

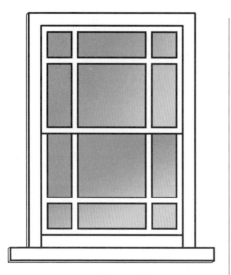

Margin light window.

format, the panes grew in size as well. The hierarchy of windows to rooms still prevailed, with the entrance of the home traditionally being in a middle floor, accessed by steps up to the main entrance. The Georgian era is also characterised by symmetry, not just with windows but chimneys and details as well.

Brickwork walls were built perhaps one and a half or two bricks thick at the basement and ground levels, but were reduced to one brick thick for the upper floors. Soft local stock bricks and thin lime mortar joints are typical façades, but note that experienced bricklayers were often employed to build the outer face, and apprentices the inner. Consequently, the inner walls tend to have thicker bed joints, and there is no bond between the two.

19th century

A lot of Victorian architecture remains with us today, partly thanks to the house building boom of that era and the sound construction methods and durable materials they employed. But like us, the Victorians were keen on using the architectural styles of the past and replicated them at the lower end of the housing market.

From 1838 glass could be rolled instead of being cast and became cheaper, leading to bigger window panes and the use of stained glass in doors and window lights. The 1840s saw a Queen Anne revival period, with softer red bricks (known as rubbers) being popular and lime putty joints winning out over stone or stucco. Feature hoods over windows also reappeared in this retro period – all good, solid design ideas that reflected the mood of the era.

In 1860 the Victorians moved onto Gothic Revival, the style with pointy arched windows and spired roofs. This era also saw the prolific use of fishtail tiles on roofs in some regions, and on terraced and semi-detached urban homes, columns were used in the

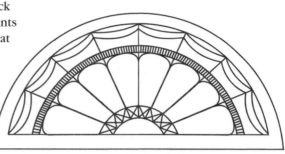

Leaded decorative fanlight (18th century).

corners of the bay windows, usually prefabricated and available from the local builder's merchants, which explains why once in a while you see two that don't quite match. I can see the labourer coming back with them on the horse and cart, saying, 'Well, that's all they had in stock, Guv.' You also see dentil courses and sometimes brackets under the eaves, and arches that have cast features over the entrance doors.

The 1875 the Public Health Act controlled a boom in the mass house-building market with streets of narrow-fronted terraced homes. Semi-detached homes first appeared in the late part of this century.

The 1880s saw the arrival of the Arts and Crafts movement, which made a complete fuss over everything, including the architecture of houses. White render over dark walls was used to carve out patterns, surprisingly often involving naked cherubs (they were very keen on naked cherubs in the 1880s – couldn't get enough of them) and fancy roof coverings of double pantile clay tiles were laid to shallow rafters. In all, this was very decorative stuff that kicked sand in the face of the standard designs of the time.

Building materials could be shifted around the country a lot easier with the coming of the railways in the middle of this century. This meant that materials needn't be indigenous and methods vernacular to that area, so basically you saw the same houses all over the country then, much as we see the same street scenes now.

20th century

Cavity walls were introduced at the beginning of the century, the very first dating from 1901. At the time builders were using snap headers to give the appearance of Flemish bond in a solid wall construction, so be warned: the wall may look solid, but could well be two skins of brickwork in a cavity construction. This was the Queen Anne revival again, as all brickwork dating from Anne's reign was Flemish bond; English bond took over later. Generally speaking, Edwardian architecture didn't fool around too much with retro ideas and things, but there are subtle differences: for example, sash windows are usually framed by more slender sections than thicker Victorian sashes.

The First World War put a stop to house-building for the duration, and it was not until the 1920s and 1930s that things started to pick up again. 1923 brought the International style of architecture, although only to a few people who could afford it. The look is very modernistic, with square, boxy shapes and curved windows, a lot employing reinforced concrete to create cantilevers and so forth. Unfortunately, the architecture was a bit ahead of the technology, particularly the concrete technology of the time, and this fact has given rise to structural problems since then with some of this era's buildings, not least Frank Lloyd Wright's riverside classic, 'Falling Water', in Pennsylvania, USA, which for a while looked like it might live up to its name, if not in the way that its architect intended.

The recession of 1929–33 meant that not much was built. To make up for the years of mass unemployment, mass housing estate schemes got things going again in 1933–34. Metal windows were now being used and can be dated to some extent by whether or not they are galvanised: the process started after 1945, and before this steel was bare and painted direct. 1930s homes may also have some of the Art Deco style of the period, with curved bay windows and stained glasswork; oriel windows were also popular at this time. In many Art Deco-style homes, the period details usually extend right through the home from the stair balustrading to the stained glass windows and the internal doors – all of them distinctive.

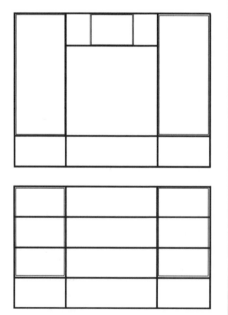

Two examples of typical metal window fenestration (20th century).

Between the end of the recession and beginning of the war in 1939, some speculative property development occurred, and in well-constructed bungalows and two-storey homes from this period fully hipped and close-boarded roofs were common, as were large bay windows with supporting corner posts, some of which have suffered at the hands of replacement-window companies in more recent years.

After 1945 the term 'home improvement' was unlikely to be heard – home survival was more common, and it was a case of having to use what resources you had to get by. Many homes saw original features like balusters and window shutters removed for firewood. These were hard times, and Britain saw little new house-building until the early 1950s. The Festival of Britain in 1951 led a drive to trying to get the country back on its feet, and brought many new materials and ideas with it: for instance, plywood had been used in aircraft-building during the war, and was now introduced to home-building and furniture.

System-built homes, such as the first steel-framed properties, were introduced, and precast concrete features also popped up at the time in window and door surrounds, as well as in concrete panel walls designed for quick construction. These homes are known as cross-wall construction homes and are quite different structurally from conventionally built ones: the internal walls are critical to the stability of the others and the floors above, and alterations, such as forming openings between rooms, are difficult, if not actually impossible to achieve. No-fines concrete also became popular after the war and remained so for many years – indeed, Wimpey Homes built thousands with this method between 1945 and 1967. Only at the end of the 20th century did problems come to light with this method, and many of these properties have now been demolished.

In the 1950s ceiling heights dropped and rooms became multi-use. The kitchen/diner was born and instantly changed the engine-room convention of the kitchen as a separate place that shouldn't be seen into the rest of the home, where it should. Kitchens might have appeared, but something else disappeared at the same time – the chimney, or at least the fireplace. As a focal point in living rooms it had been replaced by something smaller and boxlike – the TV. Allegedly the nation's perspective dropped a few degrees when this happened, and nobody noticed the fact that people were building houses with lower ceilings.

In the 1960s terraces of homes with trussed rafters appeared for the first time. At this stage, 'new and modern' was desired, not old or even renovated, and older homes from Georgian or Victorian times fell into dereliction. Many were given closing orders and were marked as unfit for human habitation; the postwar years had left them unmaintained, and for many, restoration was beyond the owner's means. Home improvement

did start to become popular in this decade, but it came with the advent of power tools and DIY and in the form of modernisation. Modernising meant ripping out period features like old fireplaces and covering over panel doors with hardboard to give them a stylish, flush, painted finish. Of course what everybody really wanted was a brand-new trussed-rafter home with pitch-fibre drains, factory-made windows and flush hardboard-finished doors, but a new home then cost five times what an old Victorian or Edwardian home would have done.

The easiest way to determine the age of a home built since the 1970s is by the insulation – not the stuff that goes in the loft, but the insulation of the walls. Standards have changed regularly, and with each one comes a change in the cavity wall construction and its increasing thermal resistance, right up to today. My 1985 house has a 125 mm thermal lightweight block with a brick outer leaf (imperial-sized London Brick Company facings) that create a U value of 0.59 to meet the maximum 0.60 standard of the time. Bricks went metric shortly after this, and the U-value standards went up in steps to where they are today.

The house also has (though you can't see it) foundation depths governed by NHBC guidance for building near trees, and a precast concrete beam and block ground-floor structure that was first used in that decade. Modern homes might look all the same, but it will be possible to date them in the future using their materials and construction as a guide.

CHAPTER TWO

Getting Started

Materials

Given a busy building industry and a DIY industry that matches it without the fluctuations, you would think that finding everything you need would be a doddle, wouldn't you? It isn't. Time and effort have to be spent in greater quantities than you might imagine to find exactly what you want at a price you can afford. Maybe it's because the building materials industry is too big for its own good, but perhaps also it has a lot to do with merchants and large DIY chains who supply only what they supply and prefer it if you think nothing else is available.

I've said it before and I'll say it again: builder's merchants are strange places. Many are staffed by people with no knowledge of products or how they should be used and whose main purpose is to sell you something that they have, rather than something that you want, at a price you can't afford. The system of pricing is a bartering system, which exists, as far as I know, in no other shops in the UK. Builders who have accounts can, if they buy enough throughout the year, get considerable discounts on standard stuff like timber and plasterboard. When they're not paying attention 100 per cent of the time, however, they are periodically ripped off on other goods because they haven't the time to shop around. Shopping around is what you have to do if you want to avoid being robbed, particularly if you don't have a trade account and are buying in relatively small quantities.

You can't expect to walk into a builder's merchants off the street and simply buy what you want at a fair price and go away with it. There are a number of reasons why this is impossible. The first is that in all likelihood they won't have what you want in stock; think of them as a shop window displaying a selection of what is ultimately available. If they do, you'll be invited to pay through the nose for it, and third, if it's too big to carry, the delivery of goods is often charged disproportionately and optimistically for what they call small orders – bags of cement, for example, will be much cheaper from DIY superstores unless you are buying in bulk and 'negotiating' a discounted price that brings it down to its true cost.

The other thing about visiting builder's merchants is that you need to allow plenty of time – they are the exact opposite of fast food outlets. Take timber, for example: you will invariably need to track down somebody in the yard, persuade them to find what you're looking for and give you a ticket for it, so that you can take the ticket to the store counter and wait to be served in the long queue of builders passing wind and the time of day. Only after paying can you go back out to the yard and see about getting the timber to your car before the sun sets. At one merchants near me, they complete the experience by stopping you at the gate (a few yards from where you parked), searching your car and checking your receipt before you leave, just to add that extra bit of customer satisfaction that you might have missed out on until then.

I'm sure there are merchants where you can walk in, converse intelligently with the staff and be served expediently, but I've yet to meet them, and to be fair, that isn't how they go about their business. They do that by having a staffed office of estimators pricing the materials in lists for their regular customers or by taking telephone orders for delivery to them. As a member of the public, your purpose is to reconcile these discounts by paying much more. The best way to avoid this is by faxing or e-mailing lists of your material quantities to them and inviting them to price and come back to you with the best they can do. If you send the list out to as many as you can and give them a week or two to return them, you should get some idea of the game.

Wherever you can, it usually pays to use specialist merchants – plumber's merchants, for example – but again, be wary of their pricing, as it can be quite imaginative. Decorator's merchants are another specialist, as are electrical merchants; the latter are my favourite, as they don't seem to be so keen to rip off non-account holders and usually price their goods fairly. More to the point, they are helpful and swift at serving; my only problem is that if I have to order something, they never ring to say the goods are in. Not once. Clearly they have a system that relies on you continually calling in to check if it's there.

Timber merchants are another speciality supplier, and these places often have their own sawmills and grading centres where structural timber can be inspected, graded and stamped. Price-wise they can usually undercut the other general merchants in the area by dealing in bulk and storing much more, if not actually supplying the rest. They also will have sizes of timber that you can't buy anywhere else, and this alone makes them worth contacting.

If you're not careful with timber, however, you can get what you pay for – and some of it may be wet from treatment, greener than you would care for and bent as a banana. You need to check the delivery of timber as it comes off the lorry and leave on it what isn't fit.

Salvaging materials

In some areas architectural salvage has unfortunately been used as a laundry for architectural theft, and many original roof tiles and the like have been relocated from remote roofs on flat-bed trucks overnight. If you can't be sure where your reclamation yard is reclaiming materials from, then it would be wiser to look for new 'traditional' materials. There is a growing market for handmade and traditional materials, from stone tiles to ironwork door furniture and blown glass. If it's used and appreciated, not only will it become cheaper and more widespread, but thieves won't have the opportunity to rob the past.

You may be able to re-use materials from your home: bricks can be cleaned up, tiles carefully lifted off and glass removed from rotten windows, so don't automatically throw things in the skip. Aim to remedy badly carried out repairs and alterations; for example, raking out cement mortar joints to lime-mortar brick walls and repointing them with lime mortar will not only improve the appearance of the wall but also help to protect the soft bricks and keep the wall flexible.

Lime in period homes

I can think of no other material that has survived extinction solely because of restoration work. We pretty much stopped using lime in favour of cement some decades ago, and nobody seemed to notice. Until now.

Lime putty is most commonly used for repointing old walls today where lime mortar exists, because typically the joints are thinner and the colour whiter due to lime mortar, and any attempt to try to match it with cement will look disastrous. As well as repointing walls or using it as a mortar bedding for new brickwork, lime can also be mixed with selected sand or stone dust and used to repair stonework. It can also be used in specialist stone-cleaning methods.

The real advantage of lime mortar in construction, particularly in the mortar bedding of bricks, lies in its flexibility, which can be a definite advantage in older homes built from shallow foundations. Movement in older buildings will show up if rigid methods of reconstruction are used, and cement mortar can be brittle and prone to cracking. Lime mortar remains soft and mastic-like, and absorbs movement from seasonal changes in the subsoil without showing damage.

Because lime is more porous than the bricks it surrounds, it can allow some movement of moisture and allow the wall to breathe. Breathable construction is recognised as good construction these days, and walls that allow vapour to permeate out are considered to last much longer and are less prone to damage in winter. While keeping the weather out, you must be careful not to seal up the home and trap moisture in. We generate large amounts of moisture as water vapour in everyday living, and this needs to escape through the building continuously. Permeable, or breathable if you prefer, construction allows this to happen.

Be aware, however, that lime also comes bagged and labelled as 'hydraulic lime', which you can regard as impure. It contains silica and alumina since it's derived from impure limestone, and has been more commonly used in modern construction because it sets faster and harder than pure lime. Cement mortar mixes you see described as 1:1:6, for example, refer to one part hydraulic lime, one part cement and six parts sand. Really they are designed for cavity wall methods, where more rigid construction is needed.

Material claims

It's an annoying trend that shows no sign of stopping, but manufacturers of home-improvement materials are prone to claiming that their products, and theirs alone, are 'required' or 'endorsed' or 'necessary' to meet the requirements of the Building Regulations and other laws of the industry – requirements which they wouldn't trouble you, the home-owner, with, but which you, the home-owner, will be in trouble with if you don't buy the product.

It's becoming commonplace to see full-page technical 'reports' in the trade press drawing on a particular problem or failure with buildings and resolving it with a particular product. Disguised in the shape and style of independent reports, this is 21st-century advertising. These people are trying to sell their product, and the industry has found it to be a successful way of selling – particularly where builders are concerned. Troubled by the risk of not complying, they are anxious to buy products that save them the trouble of finding solutions or alternatives. When it comes to home improvements there are always choices, and usually you could fill a bucket with them.

Only you, the home-owner, can stand in the way and refuse to rely on commercially based claims for any product or renovating technique – remember that independent advice is not available from anybody who has something to sell you.

Building Regulations

Complying with the Building Regulations is a separate matter to Listed Building Consent or Planning Permission. The regulations impose requirements that relate to the technical detail of the work you do in the interests of health and safety, energy efficiency and access for the disabled.

Although the builder or contractor carrying out the work has a responsibility for complying with the Building Regulations, you, the home-owner, are ultimately responsible. Enforcement procedures for not complying with, or for withholding a Completion Certificate will affect you and your home, not the contractor.

Much home renovation work falls under the heading of repair or restoration, and is not controlled by the regulations. However, the scope of this legislation is forever expanding, as are the performance minimums dictated. Work that is subject to control includes:

● Replacement windows

● Replacement fuel-burning appliances of any type (boilers, fires, etc.)

● The provision of services for washing and sanitation (WCs, baths, showers, washbasins and sinks, for example)*

● Hot-water cylinders

● Foul and rainwater drainage work*

● Rebuilding load-bearing walls

● Reconstructing floors

● Reconstructing roofs

- Underpinning foundations

- Electrical alterations

- Chimney construction or part removal

- Cavity wall insulation

- Relining chimneys with new flues

- Installing an oil or LPG tank outside your home

(* The extent of work in these categories may determine whether an application is required. Check with your local authority Building Control Service for advice about your proposals. Repairs to elements that can be exempted may require no alteration in the position of that element to qualify; for instance, if you re-route a broken drainage system or relocate a WC, this usually counts as new work, while replacing it in its existing position is a repair.)

Even if the renovation work does not fall under the scope of the regulations, you may wish to use the guidance documents along with other published standards, to ensure it is safe and to a reasonable quality. Work that is exempt may include:

- Repairing roof coverings

- Repairing walls

- Repairing leaking drains

- Minor electrical work

- Replacing glass in windows and doors

- Refinishing floors, ceilings and walls

- Re-insulating (other than cavity wall insulation)

- Altering fireplaces, surrounds or hearths

Building Regulation Applications
Full Plans

If you would like the full details of your work checked and approved before you start, consider a Full Plans Application. Drawings, and in some cases structural calculations, should be submitted for consideration. Building Regulations work to a statutory five-week date (which may be extended with your consent to two months). They may write to you, setting out a list of defects or amendments to the plans required before approval. Or, they may simply make these points the subject of a Conditional Approval. Either way, they should be addressed before work starts, to avoid problems on-site.

If you do intend to submit your own plans, it is quite likely that unless you are familiar with current Building Regulations and construction, they will need to be amended. If you have faith in your builder's knowledge and abilities, you may wish to avoid a Full Plans Application under the Building Regulations and submit a Building Notice (not available in Scotland).

Building Notice

This is a statement of your intention to do work and comply with the requirements of the regulations, and requires no plans or design information to be submitted. It gives your Building Control Officers 48 hours notice of your intention to start the job. They will inspect the work at various stages on notification by you or your builder, and will advise you of any problems drawn to their attention. There is a certain element of risk with the Building Notice method, because you do not have the benefit of an approved plan to work to, and the Building Control Officer may not always be able to predict what problems are ahead of you and warn you in advance. Consequently it is only advisable to adopt this procedure after discussing with your builder and Building Control Officer the scheme in detail, and only then if you are satisfied that they can agree on the details before each stage of the work.

The fees for both are usually identical, although often Building Notice fees are paid 100 per cent on submission, and Full Plans 25 per cent on submission and 75 per cent on commencement. Building Control authorities set their own fees, which vary from one authority to another.

Building Warrant (Scotland)

In Scotland you must obtain a Building Warrant before starting work. It is not possible to build at your risk by starting work in advance of receiving it. In lieu of the Approved Documents, the Scottish Regulations are documented by the Technical Standards instead.

Listed Buildings

Listed Buildings have a brief description (often a single paragraph) on the 'list' describing them and their architectural and historical attributes. A copy of the list is held by your local authority Planning Department and the National Monuments record, and may also be available for reference in your local library. The system of listing was introduced in 1950, and grades are given to each property. In England and Wales, Grades I, II* and II apply, and in Scotland and Northern Ireland Grades A, B and C apply – far more logically, it must be said.

If your home was built before 1700 and any part of it is original it should be listed, and a fair percentage of homes built between then and 1840 is also covered. After that listing becomes a little rare, and after 1945 it becomes extremely rare. If you are still not certain whether your home is listed, you can telephone the Listed Buildings Information Service or your local Planning Authority, who hold a copy of the list. Some half a million buildings are on the list, of which over 90 per cent are recorded as Grade II*. If you're fortunate enough to own a Grade I or II* property, you may be eligible for grant aid with any major repairs from English Heritage; in Northern Ireland the Ulster Architectural Society, in Scotland Historic Scotland, and in Wales Cadw (meaning keep) are guardians whose role is equivalent to English Heritage.

If your home is listed, all of it, not just the features referred to, is covered by the planning laws in this respect. Listed Building Consent is a separate entity to Planning Permission and covers a wider range of works. Internal renovations, as well as external ones, may require consent, and that includes the demolition and removal of parts of your home.

Local authorities are also able to provide grants for alteration and repair, and are not restricted to grades of buildings but are free to use their discretion. They can also be used in Conservation Areas or other special areas where owners are trying to preserve or enhance the character of their homes.

Once you've decided on what renovations you would like to undertake, it is essential to contact your local authority Conservation Officer to see whether consent is required. Included in applications, which currently attract no fee, they will wish to see architectural design details drawn to a large scale for details such as window and other joinery replacements. Conservation officers may wish to visit your home before work starts to assess your application's proposals.

Builders and specialist contractors

Home renovation is more than just improving your home for modern-day life, it's also about the process of restoring the features and character of your home. To that end, engaging a 'general builder' might not be appropriate, although it has to be said that there are those who specialise in renovation work for complete home-restoration projects. The Heritage Building Contractors Group may be able to refer you to registered members in your area.

Unfortunately, there are still plenty of unscrupulous builders who have an interest in finding faults in your home and in comparing an older property to a new one, to hike up the cost of renovation. Old homes don't comply with current Building Regulations, and never will. The only true way to guard against the escalating cost of work in renovating is to use a professional architect or surveyor to oversee the project with you. He or she will be able to inspect your home and specify the work needed to carry it out for a builder to follow.

For individual tasks, tradesmen can still be found with the skills for carrying out traditional building crafts. The Building Conservation Directory has invaluable advice in its articles, but primarily keeps a database of advisory bodies in the United Kingdom that you can use. English Heritage, the Institute of Historic Building Conservation and the Society for the Protection of Ancient Buildings also give advice, some of it free and some at cost in brochures and leaflets, on a wide range of renovation tasks.

Contingencies

With work of this nature, surprises are all too often around the corner. It isn't always possible to measure the full extent of the work while some of it is covered up. When walls come down or finishings are removed, what was lurking behind may not be in the best of health.

It is absolutely essential to have a contingency sum in your budget for dealing with these surprises because when they happen you may find yourself with a sudden lack of options. Consider this:

On a half-brick-thick ground floor partition, old damp plaster is hacked from a wall to prepare for its injection with a chemical damp-proof course. The plaster should have only been hacked off up to 1 m or so high, but was in such a bad state that what didn't fall off had to be completely removed, revealing the brickwork beneath. The bricks are poorly bonded, but worse, now stripped of their plaster, some are damaged and loose, and the wall can be moved with one hand. Will it stand up to being drilled for the damp-proofing, or does it look so bad now that it needs to be taken down and rebuilt with new materials?

It isn't just major work that can evolve; even redecorating is vulnerable – stripping off old wallpaper, layer after layer, can ultimately lead to stripping off lumps of plaster.

I don't mean to dissuade you from the task in hand. It is going to be worth knowing that your home has been professionally and effectively renovated and that it will serve you well in the future, whether you choose to live in it or sell it on, but you really do have to allow for contingencies in a renovations budget.

Dealing with problems and disputes

It's a fact of life that things go wrong from time to time, and where building works are concerned, it seems like a certainty. It helps if you can adopt a flexible frame of mind, or at least a resilient one open to the possibility of some part of your plans evolving in a way that you hadn't previously envisaged. The highest risk of dispute arises when one or both of the parties are pursuing, single-mindedly, doggedly and uncompromisingly, a particular path. Buildings, you see, are not obliged to help, and often they throw up obstacles and secrets that get in the way, and it's more likely that people will change their mind as the renovation takes shape, than the building changing shape to suit the people. Yes, it is good to be focused on the end result, but there are different ways to get there, and being focused shouldn't be confused with being blinkered. Keep an open mind and keep talking to your builders, and you'll be fine.

If a dispute does seem to be irresolvable, adjudication is the chosen method for resolving it. An adjudicator is appointed to act like a referee on written contracts, or rather contracts that have been witnessed in writing. The Housing, Grants, Construction and Regeneration Act 1996, which first set up this principle, excludes home renovation work (or any work where one of the parties resides or intend to reside) from its control, but that doesn't mean that you can't write a clause into your contract based on its principles.

The principles of adjudication

● Agree on where the adjudicator will be found. Nominated bodies like the RICS, RIBA and ABE have professional members who can act in this role.

● Serve notice of your intention to refer to adjudication on the other party or parties.

● Give a referral report to the adjudicator, detailing the nature of the dispute, together with any relevant documents.

● Invite the other party to submit a response to the referral report.

● Require the adjudicator to rule on the dispute a maximum of 28 days after receiving both parties' reports.

Because the statutory scheme lies outside domestic home improvements, the arbitrator's ruling is not enforceable through the courts under the Housing, Grants, Construction and Regeneration Act 1996. However, if it forms part of the contract between parties it can be upheld in this respect.

Renovation after flooding

If you've ever suffered from rising damp or condensation you'll probably not want to read this section. Flooding can be terminal for a home, or it can

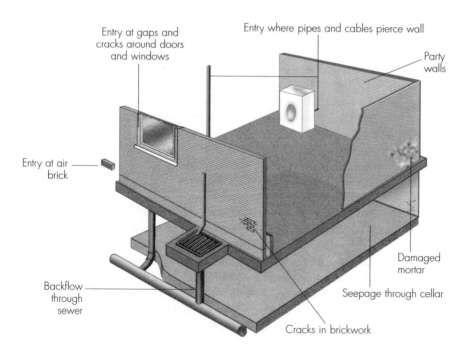

Potential entry points for flood water.

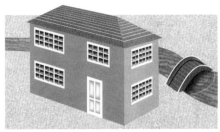

Proximity to a river

Run off from high ground

Proximity to the sea

Depression of valley floor

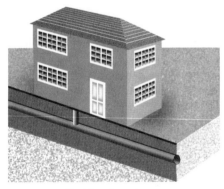

Backflow from drains

Rising groundwater

Causes of flooding.

just be very messy. Some new homes have been flooded by 1 m of water before it subsided, leaving 600 mm of mud behind and a structure that economically could only be demolished and rebuilt. Flood damage can also be reparable - it may take some time to thoroughly dry the walls and floors out and then undertake some extensive renovation afterwards, but it is fixable. If you are renovating a flood-damaged home, it is worth knowing what measures you can take, if any, to prevent it happening again.

A burst river bank, overladen drainage system or coastal tide surge

35

can bring water to your home, and bring it very quickly. The Environment Agency has areas of risk mapped and gives out coded flood warnings, but when it happens, flooding can be sudden. You might struggle to see how anything can be done to stop the damage from an event like this once the water has reached your front door, but surprisingly there are ways of limiting it, some of which appear to be very effective.

The measures can be divided into two types: those that can be built into your home permanently are known as passive measures, while those that you put in place just before a flood, as a temporary emergency measure, are positive measures.

Checklist of expert flood-defence measures

Passive measures:

REWIRE THE ELECTRICAL SYSTEM FROM THE FIRST FLOOR LEVEL DOWN

The ring main is often damaged by water ingress and requires rewiring, so this time install the cables through the first floor of your home with socket outlets positioned higher than usual (say at 1.2 m above the finished ground floor) to avoid them being flooded again. Homes with solid concrete ground floors have their ring mains run at this level anyway, but timber ground floors tend to traditionally accept the wiring from between the joists at this ground level.

Remember that since 2000 all new homes have had to have their socket outlets positioned between 450 and 1200 mm above floor level anyway, for accessibility requirements. Dropping all switches and sockets to this level from the floor above will do a lot to prevent the cost of rewiring the home after a flood.

DRAINAGE SEALING

Drains are a common point of entry for floodwater, but non-return valves can be fitted to drainage retrospectively. With stormwater drains backing up and causing much flood damage every year, fitting valves that let water out, and only out, from your home can be cost-effective. Drainage, however, lives in a system of interconnecting pipes and manholes, and if this approach is to work to protect your home you will need to ensure that all the entry points to it are secure.

This could mean replacing manhole covers with sealed and bolted-down covers as well; these are normally reserved for internal manholes as fixtures that will prevent lids being lifted up by water pressure until the water has found another outlet. Non-return valves are often used to guard the ends of storm-water sewers discharging into rivers, and will effectively stop any back flow of water up the drain.

Protecting drainage is hard, but is all the more worthwhile when your rainwater and foul systems are combined together into one system. Historically this was quite popular, and older urban homes tend to have combined drains like this, rather than the separate ones found in newer or modern homes.

USE WATER-DURABLE MATERIALS WHERE YOU CAN

So I made up the term 'water-durable', but it says what I mean: for example, chipboard, MDF, plasterboard and even thistle plaster aren't water-durable. Saturation in water destroys them to the point where they have to be replaced. I have seen the effect of vandalism on a new home, where a chipboard ground floor finish laid over insulation sheets was wrecked after a hose was fed through an open window and the water was left on. The chipboard warped and was unable to dry out in the same shape.

Solid concrete floors and hard surface finishings like screed and tiling are not permanently damaged by water, and rendered and set walls or tanked walls are also examples of water-durable materials. Do not be tempted to believe that moisture-resistant labelled products are the same: floor-grade chipboard and plasterboard can be bought now as moisture-resistant, but this only means that they can stand up to a bit of condensation – a mild dampening, not a flood.

FLOODPROOFING WALLS, WINDOWS AND DOORS

This may be a bit excessive for standard renovation work unless you are sure a flood is on the cards in the future. Flood barriers that are removable for everyday use, and that can be attached quickly when a flood warning is given, can be fitted to window and door openings. They are specialist products that form a

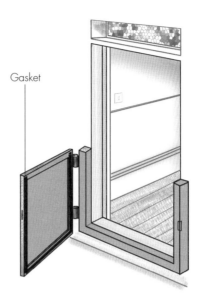

Gasket

Hinged panel across a doorway.

watertight seal at low level across openings once a permanent sealed frame is fixed to the reveals of wall openings to accept them. Because these fixtures rely on the owner being present in the house at the time of the flood warning, they are usually described as 'positive measures' rather than 'passive measures'.

The external walls of the home can be floodproofed as a passive measure with tanking that can be secured externally and is capable of resisting water pressure. Some tanking products for basements are able to this internally, where the water pressure is from the outside and is therefore negative on the tanking. Using them on the outside of the home means that the performance of these products is enhanced because the water pressure is positive, holding them to the wall. A cement-rendered finish is essential, together with a concrete surface on the surrounding ground that diverts water away.

Of course not all homes can be rendered outside, and for these, floodproof walls as garden walls that surround the home are another good solution. At 1 or 1.2 m high, a cement-rendered continuous wall with attachable gate barrier may be all that is needed to keep the rising tide at bay for long enough. If you live in a rural area and have the land, you might consider the possibility of forming earth mounds outside – natural embankments that can be turfed and planted in the garden landscape but also serve to defend your home. When constructing any external barrier, think about what will happen if any of the water breaches it – a drainage channel that gives it a route out is essential if you are to avoid the prospect of trapping the water in and creating your very own moat of rising water.

The possibility of Planning Permission being required should also be explored with your local authority. This will depend on your location and whether the area has any special designation in planning terms, such as a Conservation Area or Special Landscape Area, which might control your plans.

SUMPS AND PUMPS

Basement renovation work often includes the installation of pumps and sump holes from which water will naturally gather and can then be removed. Flood precautions in renovation work could well extend to providing a sub-floor area beneath a suspended ground floor, but whether this is possible and worthwhile will depend on your situation. The depth of the void available under the floor will have a bearing.

Getting the floorboarding up is the easy part; working between the joists to prepare the sub-floor base is not so easy if the void isn't deep enough to get beneath. The surface of the sub-base should ideally be concreted and tanked with a suitable damp-proofing membrane. If the concrete is finished to a slope that leads the water to a sump, a submersible pump can be sited in it and the water can be pumped up through plastic piping to a discharge point outside your home. Which begs another question: if the home is flooded inside, perhaps the drains outside are as well, so where do you pump the water to? The fire brigade had this problem in Folkestone once, when August floods filled the streets and homes in one part of the town. Pumping the water back out into the street was a little pointless until the water in the streets could be discharged into the harbour.

If your drains are secure and your home is more at risk from a rising water table than a burst river, then a sump and pump operated by a ball-float switch could be all you need to keep your feet dry. If electricity is not going to be safely available in this situation, the pump should be powered by a portable generator or

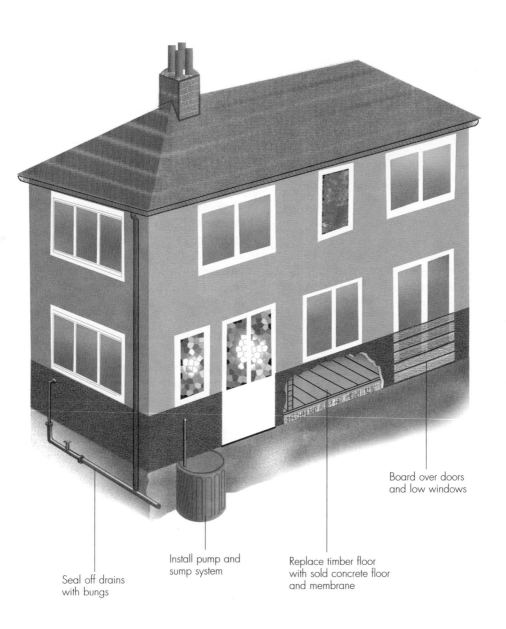

Board over doors
and low windows

Seal off drains
with bungs

Install pump and
sump system

Replace timber floor
with sold concrete floor
and membrane

Flood protection measures.

Fit temporary airbrick covers.

battery power and should be accessible through a floor trap hatch for maintenance.

Positive measures

DRAIN SEALING

I've seen advice given on the subject of emergency flood precautions that involves wedging soft balls in the drains, held in place by lumps of wood, and even removing the WC and sealing off the end of the pipe with a ball. I find it difficult to believe that anyone will be inclined to go to this extreme at the 'Blue Peter' end of flood prevention measures, but if you are inclined not to build in passive defences, then buying a few drainage test plugs will be better than stuffing balls up your drains. Drain test plugs and air bags that can be inflated by handpumps to seal off drains are commonly used for testing new drainage work, and are commonly available from builder's merchants.

They are designed to seal off pipes of this size against water pressure, so leave your kids to play with the balls.

AIR-BRICK COVERS

These are often overlooked, but of course they are water entry points in flood situations. Some specialist watertight covers can now be purchased that will fit over them, but air bricks in walls do an essential job of ventilating beneath timber floors and mustn't be covered permanently. They may also be serving as combustion air vents for fires or gas appliances, and the consequences of leaving them covered over are dire (see page 67), so these covers should be considered as positive temporary measures only.

DOORS

PVC-U doors (particularly those that open outwards, as French doors commonly do) might already form a good seal for keeping out the water. But with the addition of silicone mastic around the edge face of the door for it to close against, the water pressure of floodwater will help to form a watertight seal.

POLYTHENE

As an eleventh-hour positive measure, wrapping the lower part of your outside walls with heavy-duty polythene, such as that used for damp-proof membranes (DPMs) will do a lot to reduce water damage to walls. 1–2 m high is usually enough, but it is also worth extending the cover over the garden to prevent soil erosion or a mudslide. DPM duct tape is used for jointing the sheet.

Starting work after a flood

If you're faced with the task of renovating your home after a flood, the prospect must be daunting, but the urge to get started and bring life back to normal must also be overwhelming. Be aware that during times of flood, waters can rise and fall over a period of weeks, with the vagaries of rainfall and the drainage trying to cope with it. So don't be tempted to jump the gun and start on work that will only become damaged again quickly; instead, focus on immediate preventative measures that will see your home protected while you wait for the threat of flooding to disappear. You may also be waiting for an insurance claim to be assessed, of course.

If you are thinking about minor renovation after a flood, remember that floodwater contaminates what it touches, so all surfaces should be cleaned with disinfectant to avoid possible infections. The home will need a lot of ventilation to dry out thoroughly, and removing fixed kitchen units and cupboards will probably be needed to allow the walls behind them to dry.

CHAPTER THREE

Replacing and Restoring

Preservative and damp-proofing treatment

Just as with replacement windows, a whole industry has sprung up dealing with damp-proofing and timber decay. It was founded by valuation surveyors in the 1980s, who seemed to record on every older house sale that specialist investigation be given to the subject. They didn't mean to say that they had discovered damp or dry rot (because they hadn't actually looked) – they were just covering their backsides by requiring that somebody else should. The problem was that the somebody else was often not another independent surveyor, who would charge professional fees for a full structural survey or proper investigation, but a company who were in the business of selling preservative treatment and damp-proofing work. Their surveys were, indeed are, of course free, and along with them comes a quote for carrying out the work, which – not surprisingly – they diagnose as being necessary.

You see the problem – the mortgage lenders accepted these reports and the industry was locked into a circular self-propelling business (valued in the late 1980s at some £20,000,000 per year) that often forced home-owners into having to pay for unnecessary remedial work. It's also worth mentioning that the custodians of many historic buildings, English Heritage and the National Trust, don't generally consider injection damp-proof treatment to be necessary or of any real value in the long-term preservation of their buildings. They also shy away from the chemical treatment of timber in their properties constructed before 1930.

On the plus side you could say that damp-proofing is a good preventative measure if done properly, but on the down side you can spend a fortune introducing chemicals to your home environment that aren't needed and ignoring things that are.

Diagnosing rising damp

Traditionally, electronic meters have been used to detect dampness in walls, but surface condensation has sometimes given misguiding results. Dampness in plaster is often caused by humidity within the room, and when warm moist air meets a cold surface it condenses, creating damp and often the growth of black mould. The corners of rooms are a likely spot for the worst symptoms to show up in, but if the room hasn't been well ventilated and heated, condensation will occur.

Rising damp is something entirely different and rarer. It comes from the ground up through the foundations and into the wall structure, and as a result ground salts are often discovered in the dampness. Alas, to discover their presence involves taking samples or readings from inside the wall and not on its surface. This of course means having to damage the surface finishings and decoration, but if renovation work is going to be done this shouldn't upset you unduly.

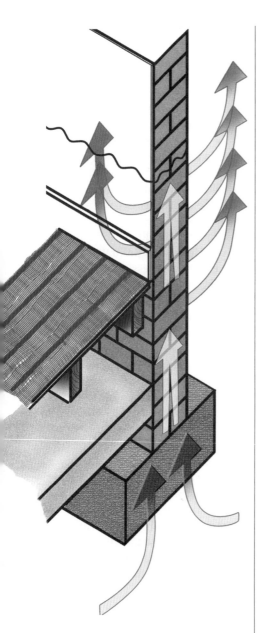

Without an effective damp-proof course, rising damp can climb walls and create a tide mark at its highest level.

A sample of the mortar from within the wall can then be taken for laboratory analysis. It requires analysis because hygroscopic salts are present in building materials anyway, although they are more obvious in the case of new buildings, where time and the rain have yet to wash them out. If you ever see a new home with white chalk like stains over the brickwork, it is due to salts in the bricks effervescing out, and only with time and rain washing will it come out and disappear. But for rising damp to be diagnosed, the salts found from within the mortar of a brick wall must contain nitrates and chlorides that are found in groundwater – proof that the damp is rising from the ground.

Measuring damp is often done using electronic resistance or capacitance meters equipped with a pair of penetrating needle-like prongs that are meant to be able to penetrate the wall and detect rising damp, assuming you can get them through the plaster. The prongs are questionably short and you can't get them through to the brickwork without drilling holes first, but then I've never been that confident about the readings they give. I don't think it wise to base a rising damp diagnosis on meter readings alone.

Damp is easy to see when it's that bad. Apart from the musty smell from just being inside a home with a damp problem, you can often see darker patches on the finishings, along with peeling wallpaper, blistering paint, rotting or splitting woodwork and the presence of mould growth. With rising damp a horizontal tide mark may even be evident, as it has crept up the wall, although traditionally the advice is that it seldom reaches higher than 1 m above ground.

Whenever studies have been done on damp problems, only a small percentage of cases are attributed to rising damp; the majority are often rain penetration, coming through the walls laterally under pressure from the wind or around windows and doors. About a third are due to condensation. Even when rising damp is assigned, this might be due to the fact that the outside ground level has been raised in the past and now bridges the DPC level – injecting the wall with a chemical will do nothing to resolve problems like these. If the ground is too high outside, the only solution is to lower it. If the brickwork in the walls is too porous it will need cladding with render, tile hanging or boarding, and so on.

Rising damp must be affected by the ground water table as well. For example, in winter clay can become waterlogged, leaving your foundations immersed for months on end, but in summer the water table can disappear to much greater depths, leaving your foundations bone dry. So rising damp is often seasonal.

Chemical injection damp-proofing

The absence or apparent absence of a damp-proof course has been enough for many homeowners to be sold a chemical injection DPC. As mentioned before, in the past government grant aid has been liberally handed out to allow properties to have this work done. After this it soon became

'necessary' for it to be 'investigated' on the sale of older homes. When I was 15 years old, we had to move out of our council home for five months to allow for renovation work to be done, and it was this chemical injection process that required the home to be unoccupied; you don't really want to be living in a property that has this stuff being pumped into the walls – the fumes are not healthy and take a few weeks to dissipate, longer to disappear.

To begin, the old plaster is hacked off to at least a height of 750 mm above any dampness (salt contamination) and the bare brickwork is exposed. The wall is then drilled with holes at specified centres and the solution is pumped in to disperse through the brickwork.

Ideally the process of replastering is done with a renovating plaster that has some water-repellancy added to the mix. With the brickwork cleaned off and treated, the first scratch coat of cement and sand render can be applied with a treatment of fatty acid soap mixed in to the water to improve its damp resistance. A second coat of render, making the depth up to about 20 mm, and finally a multi-finish or thistle finish plaster are then applied. Your specification will depend on the depth of your existing plaster, against which you will need to finish flush.

I have heard of older homes built from soft stock bricks and lime mortar – i.e. typical Georgian house construction – where damp-proofing the basement and lower walls has pushed the damp problems higher up the walls. Built from soft, flexible and breathable materials, buildings like this don't take kindly to being sealed in, so I would strongly advise you to find more sympathetic methods of dealing with damp in homes built like this.

Packaged damp treatment of this kind almost always comes with a guarantee for 20–30 years, but like all guarantees the company has to remain in existence for it to be claimed, and the warranty itself is protected by many caveats.

Chimney damp

At the other end of the home, dampness in chimneys is common. In a working chimney it might actually be due to the condensing flue gases inside the chimney, the salts from these reacting with water and cement sulphates. More likely, however, is the chance that the flashings or damp-proof courses to the chimney have become old and failed and the structure is getting wet from the top down. Chimneys are particularly prone to getting wet – something to do with them being stuck out through the roof at often the highest point of the home, I suspect. The proper damp-proofing of a chimney is something that requires some careful design and work, and advice is given on building a chimney on page 70.

The most popular cause of chimney damp, however, comes from condensation within a flue that was sealed off once it was no longer required. To avoid draughts and the unwanted arrival of soot, people have understandably wanted to seal off redundant chimneys, but without some ventilation to the flue void, condensation can bring damp. If your chimney has been sealed up a little too efficiently, you can introduce an air brick at the lower level and one at the top fitted with louvred covers and insect mesh, which should hopefully solve the problem.

Timber decay and treatment

Timber will last for ages in homes if it can avoid two plagues, fungal attack and insect attack. If you discover either of these and are reluctant to leap head-first at the Yellow Pages or a 'specialist' company, you can explore the problem with your own surveyor or builder. If you do need the services of a specialist after this, look for a company registered with the British Wood Preserving and Damp-Proofing Association (BWPDA), who will provide a detailed written report following their initial survey.

For the moment, save some money and use a penknife to probe the wood. If it is easily withdrawn without a tug, it is suffering from decay. If a slight tug is needed to free it, the wood at the point of the blade can be judged to be sound. Artist's palette knives are thin, round-bladed tools that are ideal for sliding into joints between timbers to see if there is anything joining them together. When the blade slides right through a joint, you know you have a problem – certain insects like to attack timber joints at the exposed ends of the timber.

After the initial inspection comes the questioning, which may prompt you to inspect other parts of your home and to look deeper at the damage. You can use the question prompts below as a guide to finding the cause of the damage.

● Is the damage a design failure of the original construction, such as an unvented space, timber not protected by a damp-proof course, roof too flat, etc.?

● Have air bricks been covered over?

● Has the DPC been covered by raised ground finishes or rendered over ?

● Is the damage due to lack of maintenance and repair – a leaking rainwater pipe, broken drain or slipped roof tiles, for example?

● Do the same conditions exist in another area of the home where decay has not been revealed?

● Is it possible to repair the defects and then treat the damaged area?

● What finishes will have to be redone to carry out the work?

● Can the nature of the attack be specified? Is it wet or dry rot? Insect infestation?

Wet rot

All you need do to cure your home of wet rot is to keep out the wet. This occurs when some part of the building leaks and is continually saturated, and solving the damp problem will solve the rot. You may have to replace or strengthen wet-rot-affected timber if it has been left for too long, as it could well be weakened. Keep a close eye on the site as the wood dries; it may develop dry rot in doing so when it passes through the susceptible moisture content range of 20–40 per cent. If allowed to dry out to the normal 10–16 per cent moisture content of dry home timber, any dry rot should die off.

Dry rot

A fungus, dry rot not only attacks wood but also brickwork, and given the right conditions, it will spread. Oddly, the right conditions are damp ones, as it only survives in timber that has a moisture content above 20 per cent, so finding the cause of the dampness and resolving it is a key part of the cure.

The cause could be dampness beneath a suspended ground floor, where the ventilation is poor or non-existent; it could be dampness from a leaking roof or flashing – the important thing is to find the cause before concentrating on the cure; you do not want the problem to re-occur later. Even without removal or chemical treatment, once the source of damp has been removed dry rot should begin to die, and if you have a year or two at your disposal you may find it eradicates itself naturally. No, it isn't worth waiting.

Dry rot attacks most timbers, particularly softwoods – but not oak – and you can safely assume that it is easier to get than to get rid of. Both chemical treatment and the demolition hammer are typically used to eradicate it - chemical treatment, by spraying preservative over the remaining parts of the structure, only applies after the affected parts have been demolished. Start by cutting away the diseased wood and removing it. This will need to be burnt off-site - you can't save this by spraying. The timber should be cut back to 1 m beyond the infected parts, and the remaining timber should be treated with preservative, as dry rot is a good traveller and is quite happy to work its way behind plaster and around to other parts of the building away from the origin.

Determining how far dry rot has advanced is all-important. If it's been left unchecked for some time, this could spell disaster. Since all infected timber needs to be cut out and burned, some thought has to go into what replaces it and how it is installed. It isn't just wood that is affected by dry rot: brickwork can also be affected, and should be treated by sterilising. It may be possible to spray on to the wall surface, alternatively, you may need a series of irrigation holes drilled into the wall at 300 mm centres for a pumped-in application. Old bricks can be damaged by this kind of work, so it should only be considered if the structure of the brickwork is otherwise hard and sound. Some builders have been known to attack dry rot with a blow lamp, which, apart from being highly dangerous, is also ineffective, so resist the urge to torch it.

Insect attack

It's more accurate to say that insects live with us than that we live with them. About 60 per cent of all life on Earth is insect life, and about one third of that 60 per cent is beetles. It has been said that God must have an inordinate fondness for beetles - nobody knows just how many species of them exist, but it must be millions; already there are more types of beetle known to science than there are species of plants.

It isn't really surprising, then, to discover that from time to time they choose to live in our homes. It doesn't help knowing this, because some insects can destroy key structural elements in our homes given enough time.

There are four principal suspects: furniture beetle, wood weevil, lyctus beetle and death watch beetle, and identifying which you have is best done by an expert. As well as determining which species, the expert should also be able to tell you whether the boreholes are the result of recent activity or old. Of the suspects, the death watch beetle is the worst - it removes a lot of wood in its natural activities and prefers to work in dark, undetectable areas like roof wall plates and beam ends, where it can do a lot of structural damage unnoticed.

Preservative treatment

The nature and use of chemical preservatives mean they are not for everyone. With chemicals such as copper, chrome or arsenic salts in their arsenal, they are designed to kill most biological organisms. As a form of control, they are pretty indiscriminate, in that they will protect against all forms of future attack.

The most effective method is to inject preservative under pressure, but it can be sprayed or brushed on. It'll take a while for the timber to dry out after being treated with a water-borne treatment that saturates the wood. I mention this because of the issues surrounding timber drying out and the changes to its volume that can occur when it does. A drier form of treating wood is by vacuum applying solvent-borne chemicals. Under vacuum pressure the preservative is driven into the timber and avoids the drying-out process. As good as it is, any sawn ends and knots have to be treated on-site by brush if it is to be fully protected.

Most preservative has an insecticide element that, when surface-applied (brushed or sprayed on), will kill off any larvae or adult beetles residing inside. Unfortunately, water-borne treatment doesn't tend to soak very far into timber, and hence only works against the emerging bugs as they come out to begin life or catches the adults going in to lay their eggs.

Organic solvent-borne preservative penetrates a lot further and offers much longer-term protection. If you have big old beams that need to be treated, it would be better to drill into a hidden surface and inject a chemical paste that will release its poison over a long period of time. If you're thinking that it sounds horrible, it's because it is. While the effect of insecticide on beetles is known, we have no idea of the effect on human health. I suspect it can't be good.

You might want to weigh the threat of living with beetles against that of living with chemicals – their being released into your home may be worse. Perhaps where possible, we should put aside the preservative and instead cut out and replace an infested beam or joist. This solution might be the easiest to live with.

Windows and doors
Windows into the past
Go back far enough in time, and windows disappear altogether. Without glass, having a hole in the wall may have been nice for light and ventilation, but it had serious consequences for security and weather resistance. On the Scottish Western Isles you can still see to this day windowless 'black houses' that are thought to closely resemble Neolithic stone homes and cone-shaped stone houses of the Dark Ages.

It's this lack of weather resistance from unglazed windows that first gave rise to the name 'wind-eyes' or 'wind-holes', later evolving to windows. In the Middle Ages, when glass was first made it was seldom used because of the expense. To help overcome this problem a variety of other materials were used to cover the wind-hole, from oiled cloth and paper to wattle without the daub. Eventually this gave way to shutters fixed over the inside of the opening. Glazed windows first appeared in 16th-century churches and large manor houses.

Metal windows, made from charcoal-smelted wrought iron,

appeared at this time too, and were valuable enough to be bequeathed and handed down through the generations. Until 1599 homebuyers often moved into a property minus its windows, which had gone with the seller, so thank your lucky stars that this isn't still done.

Metal windows fell from grace, but reappeared in the early 20th century, in particular at the end of the First World War, when steel, factory-made frames became popular. Metal windows have continued to be manufactured and used, and at least one major manufacturer has a busy trade in maintaining its century-old products. If you have metal windows to renovate, the work may have to include cutting out rusted sections and welding in new pieces, or shotblasting surface corrosion away and applying rust-prevention coatings, such as powdered zinc, as a form of cold galvanising.

Sash windows

Sash windows, originally known as 'shassis' windows, emerged in about 1670 in large properties. At first, the upper sections were often fixed and the lower sliding sash was held open with wooden pegs. The glass panes were small and the glazing bars were thick. Those seen in most homes today are Victorian or Edwardian, and are either divided into six panes per sash, creating the typical six-over-six pattern, or four panes per sash, creating the four-over-four one. Eventually, however, glass panes became larger and their numbers fell

to two over two and one over one. Without glazing bars dividing the window, some strength is lost, and sash horns were added to strengthen the sash frame.

You may be lucky enough to have margin-light sashes in your early-19th-century home. Made up of unequal panes, smaller corner lights were often formed from coloured or decorated glass. If the glass has subsequently been changed for clear float glass in these, re-glazing them with a deep primary-coloured glass would be both appropriate and enjoyable.

Timber-frame windows

Plastic windows may represent the vast majority of replacements, but PVC-U is not an option. In Conservation Areas, or simply where a more sustainable material is wanted, timber is used. The cheap 'off the shelf' softwood windows used in home-building in the 20th century have given timber joinery a bad name, but purpose-made replacements in quality softwood or hardwood can be installed and will last for 30 years or more.

Apart from the aesthetic benefits, wood has the advantage of being more solid than plastic and more able to resist deformation. Because plastic doors in particular can be sprung off the latch, multi-point locking systems are needed for security. Wood, on the other hand, doesn't deform when shoulder-charged and provides a stronger fixing for screws and fastenings like door chains. This also helps prevent large window casements from being twisted out of square.

Our reasons for replacing windows in the first instance are usually maintenance ones; the existing timber frames need repainting, and perhaps the job has been left for too long and the wood is beginning to rot. The 'maintenance-free' image that plastic has acquired seems like the answer, but really it is the paint system that has failed, rather than the timber. Traditional paints sealed in the wood, preventing moisture from getting out, but in time the paint cracked and flaked away. Permeable paint systems allow the timber to breathe through micropores and hence increase its durability – not to the point of never requiring redecoration, but extending its life expectancy significantly. If you're still recoiling at the thought of ever having to repaint windows again, plastic or coated-metal windows are the ones for you.

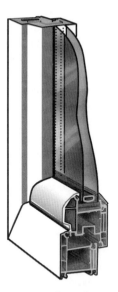

A cross section through a PVC-U window reveals that it is weaker than timber.

PVC-U windows

Since the 1980s PVC-U has become the product for window replacement. Sold on the basis that the windows are maintenance-free and there for life, the nation has fallen in love with them. 'Maintenance-free', however, stretches the truth a bit too far. For one thing, the glass in double-glazing has a definite shelf life, which can be surprisingly short at the cheaper end of the market. Double-glazing has a cavity that is now typically 20 mm wide between the panes, and is hermetically sealed around the edges; these seals tend to break down and moisture gets into the cavity, resulting in the windows misting up, and only

one solution exists when this happens – replace them. Most of the cost in this product now derives from the glass, and re-glazing a window may not be significantly cheaper than the cost of replacing one.

If you hear criticism of plastic windows based on this problem, remember that double-glazed timber windows suffer the same fate – it is the glass that is at fault. One leading rooflight company re-glazed its old windows for a while free of charge to anyone who suffered this problem.

Another common fault comes from the sliding mechanism in the scissor hinges. Plastic pins that can be tightened for friction resistance slide along a steel channel until they break in two, bringing the casement out of square with the frame.

These maintenance issues are redeemable, but compare how many companies you know in the window-maintenance business with how many you know in the window-replacement business. Plastic windows have become disposable, and clearly this needs to change. If after 30 years or so, windows do have to be replaced, let us hope that the product can be recycled without too much energy being burnt – the prospect of a plastic window mountain building up is not a pleasant one.

Certification, FENSA and Building Control

The FENSA (Fenestration Self-Assessment Scheme) system was created in April 2002, when Building Regulations were amended to include this work. The industry had been more or less unregulated before then.

To avoid the prospect of having every replaced window in the country inspected by council Building Control Officers, the industry brought in the FENSA scheme as a self-certification system by which companies could regulate themselves and avoid having to make applications for Building Regulation Approval.

Before signing any contract with a builder or window company, make sure that they show you details of their FENSA registration; if not, find out what the costs of a Building Regulation notice for the project. You can verify registration or search for a registered company on the FENSA website, or by phoning them. See Useful Contacts on page 172.

Which Building Standards apply to replacement windows and doors ?

Insulation against heat loss
The conservation of fuel is the main driving force behind controlling replacement windows and doors. Along with its introduction came higher standards for glazing in windows and doors: plastic and timber windows had their maximum U-value requirements increased to 2.0W/sq m deg K, and metal windows were relaxed to 2.2, due to the cold-bridging of their frame materials. These standards are set to rise again and will probably continue to do so.

This was a significant jump forward that effectively meant everybody had to have the best glazing available – low-e coated and with a 20 mm cavity between panes – but since then windows with argon-gas filled cavities for even better insulation have become commonly available, and these can achieve U-values as low as 1.6, the same as a 215 mm-thick brick wall. When positioned correctly in double-glazed units, low-e coatings reflect the heat trying to escape from your home back in. They are normally located on the cavity face of the inner pane and accordingly are marked to tell the installer which way round to put them (without an optical glass detector it is difficult to see if they are in right, so check before the labels are removed).

Structural stability
Replacing the windows shouldn't weaken your home, but it has been known to happen. In the past,

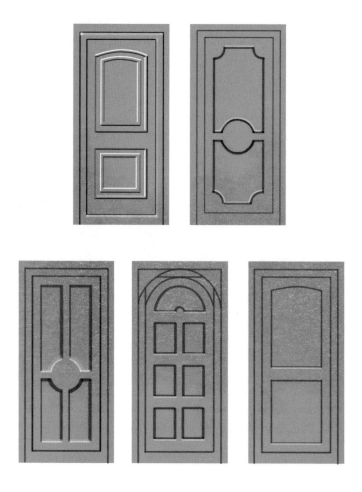

Typical PVC-U door styles.

installers have made 'adjustments' to the structural stability of a window opening when changing the window, mainly in the case of bay windows, where they have removed the structural corner posts, believing them to be part of the window frame and omitting to replace them.

I've had a few conversations with installers along the lines of plastic windows not being designed to carry load and needing to be installed beneath proper lintels like any other window. Some installers have tried to promote the idea that the nominal metal sections inside their plastic frames were super-strong and load-bearing, whereas in fact they are only designed to stiffen what would otherwise be quite a weak material for a window or door frame. The weight of structure above, even a bay window roof, must be supported by lintels and if need be posts.

Plastic window frames can't be used to carry the weight of parts of the building; in most bay windows, corner posts need to be designed to do this job, and existing beams or lintels have to be maintained over the opening. If adequate support isn't there at present, it is worth thinking about how it could be introduced before you decide that it isn't needed at all.

The exception here is some small bay window roofs that are part of the integral unit of PVC-U with a small lightweight roof. It is the windows that carry floors, walls or independent roof structures, bay or otherwise, that are the issue here.

Safety glazing

Along with the standards for thermal insulation come those for safety glass. This is a standard all about glass resisting breakage or breaking safely, aimed particularly at preventing children from serious injury.

Windows that are replaced within 800 mm of the floor and glazed doors and sidelights have to be replaced with safety glazing. Laminated or toughened glass is the preferred option, but it may be possible to use tempered or annealed glass in certain situations. The old British Standard for labelling safety glass gave it an A, B or C rating, based on swinging a pendulous weight at the pane, and

whenever glass manufacturers wanted to demonstrate their products they dropped heavy balls on them, but the new European Standard has a bit more technology in the testing. The low-level zones where the standards apply are thus referred to as 'critical zones', and it is of no consequence to the law enforcers that the window you are replacing had nothing but standard glass in it. This requirement and the one on thermal insulation are aimed at improving on what was there before.

To reap the full benefit of changing your windows and doors, you should also improve on fire safety and ventilation aspects where you can.

Fire safety

Being able to escape from windows, particularly bedroom and inner room windows, comes as a godsend. Many replacement windows in the 1980s and 1990s reduced the amount of openable area. This was partly due to the fact that plastic windows have thicker frames and mullions, coupled with friction-stay hinges that came as standard. These were of a scissor-hinge type that slid the casement into the opening a bit as it opened, with the selling point that you could safely clean the outside of the glass from the inside. It is a selling point, but this often left an opening that you couldn't get out of in a fire. Today, most windows are fitted with hinges that allow a full opening but can also be slid in to allow cleaning. These are known as 'escape-type' hinges – be sure to ask for them if they don't come as standard.

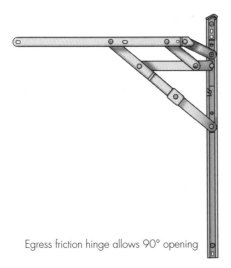

Egress friction hinge allows 90° opening

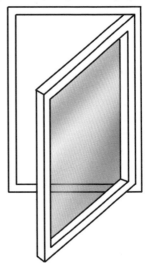

Egress friction hinge side-hung opening

Examples of egress friction hinge windows.

Ventilation

As with fire safety, ventilation should not be reduced by the replacement of a window. Rooms typically need openable areas that equal at least 20 per cent of the floor area, and if yours have this you won't have a problem. They also benefit from background (trickle) vents that are supplementary to the openable parts of the window. These small frame vents are cut into the head of the frame and allow background air to filter into the house through insect mesh. At about 10 mm wide, the slots are narrow enough to mean that even if the vents were unscrewed, burglars would be unable to use them to break into the house.

That said, however, window companies have been charging extra for trickle vents, enough to steer people away from them. As an alternative the companies have been promoting 'crack vent' fittings that allow a window to be locked slightly ajar, and windows tend to come with this feature as standard. It is often a feature of the ironmongery that it forms a two-position stay or a single-position one, which also provides background ventilation – but the manufacturers neglect to warn people of the security risk from these: a jemmy bar fits nicely into a casement or fanlight that is held ajar by a crack vent like this, and with enough leverage the window could be forced fully open.

Ventilation is also needed for fires and appliances like cookers and boilers that aren't room-sealed. If you

Scissor hinge side-hung opening (not suitable for egress)

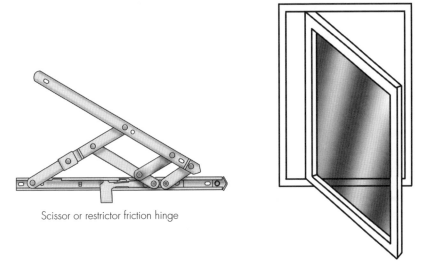

Scissor or restrictor friction hinge

Examples of scissor hinge windows.

reduce the amount of ventilation to a room with any of these features, you may do so disastrously. Without combustion air, carbon monoxide can become a life-threatening presence that is undetectable to our senses (see page 65).

Comparing costs and insurance

Included in any estimate or quote for replacement windows or doors (whether for a single window or door or the entire house) should be the fee for Building Regulation compliance. FENSA members tend to spread the cost of their membership over all their work by charging a standard fee per contract. Non-FENSA members, who will have to have their work checked by the local authority Building Control section, add the local authority fees to

each job; these are usually based on the value of the contract read against a table of charges. The latter have proved more expensive on a job-by-job basis – but the work is inspected.

Even with the FENSA scheme, the installers must notify FENSA of the work, and this information is transferred to the records of the local Building Control authority. They are also required to offer you insurance before they start the job, but you don't have to accept it. Insurance takes the form of a money-back warranty if the installers cease to trade or if there are defects with the materials or workmanship. Since the warranty should be independent, it is worth taking it out if you can afford to.

Use this checklist when inspecting the finished work of any contractor

APPEARANCE

● Are windows and doors fitted square, upright and plumb? Use a spirit level to check.

● Are the exposed parts undamaged? The protective plastic film should only have been removed once all the work is finished.

● Is the surrounding opening undamaged inside and out?

● Are there any cracks in the welds of the windows?

● Are all internal and external trims fitted correctly?

● Has all debris been removed, and has the area been left clean?

● Do the windows or doors align as required?

GLASS

● Is the glass fitted compliant with Building Regulations and as specified?

● Are the sealed units intact and neither cracked or leaking?

● Is the obscured glass correctly orientated?

● Are the low-e glass units fitted the right way around?

SEALS

● Are all the joints sealed smoothly, continuous and correctly shaped?

● Are the surrounding walls and frames free from any excess sealant? Using mastic sealant correctly is a skilled job.

FUNCTION

● When doors are slammed, is there any bounce in the mullion or outer frames? This can only be eliminated by correct installation.

● Are all drainage channels correctly positioned? Door frames can't be reversed to open the other way if drainage channels drain internally.

BAY WINDOWS

● There should be no settling of the structure when the temporary supports are removed; their purpose was not to 'jack up' the opening but to support it adequately.

● Flashings or DPCs should not have been disturbed or damaged. If they have, they should have been replaced.

Previously replaced windows and doors

The start date of 1 April 2002 applied to these controls, so if you've already had some windows replaced in your home, they will need to have been done before this date to avoid the controls. If you've had even one window or door replaced since then without certification, you should apply for a Regularisation Certificate from your local Building Control authority. They become essential when you try to sell or remortgage the place.

There is a grey area, and you might need to enter it – if contracts were signed with installers before 1 April 2002 for a job starting after that date, they didn't need to comply if the work was completed before 1 July 2002. This gave some leeway for windows that had yet to be designed for compliance with the new standards.

In practice, most medium-to-large installers of windows have become FENSA-registered. Smaller companies and general builders who undertake this work sporadically alongside other building works may not be registered, and in these cases you need to apply for Building Regulations approval.

DIY window replacement
Removing old windows
Perhaps the most stressful part of replacing window frames is getting the old ones out without doing too much damage to the surrounding decor. It's a job that can be done carefully or with a lot of ready-mix plaster, and not surprisingly, there are replacement window companies who prefer the latter. Some damage is inevitable, but this can be minimised.

Before starting, running a sharp knife around the inner face of the old frame should help to save the plaster when it's removed. Any opening casements or sashes should then be removed with the hinges and complete with the glass. The glass in fixed panes needs to come out next,

using a glasscutter and working down from the top of the pane. Once the glass is safely removed the frame can be cut out. Transoms and mullions can

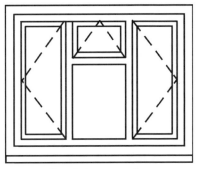

Step 1: Remove sashes.

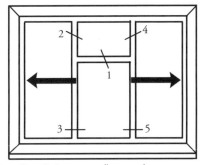

Step 2: Remove mullions and transoms.

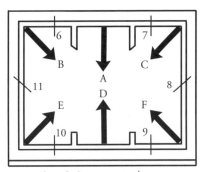

Step 3: Remove outer frame.

Removing old windows.

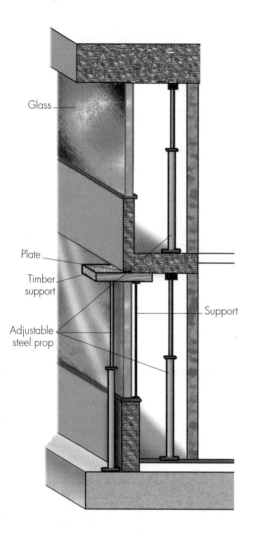

Glass

Plate

Timber
support

Adjustable
steel prop

Support

Temporary support for bay window removal.

and should be removed using a nail bar, a wooden block and some care – this is the bit where damage can be done to the surrounding plaster.

Metal windows, such as PVC-U ones, are screwed into the walls with frame fixing type screws, and will need to be either unscrewed or drilled out to release the frame. Even purpose-made zinc-coated screws don't last forever and will eventually rust, so when you choose a frame-fixing screw for new windows, choose a good-quality one – stainless steel is an excellent material for frame fixings.

The old window's horns and cills may be built in and will need to be carefully prised out from brickwork and plaster. Bay windows can't be removed without temporary steel props being installed first to support the structure, both inside and out. Replacing the bay poles or posts is the first task to be undertaken before replacement windows can be fitted.

DIY fitting

One of the problems with plastic windows is the size of the frames, which are often much thicker than the original timber ones. Edwardian and Victorian sash windows had frames that were more slender, and if you intend to replace them with plastic, albeit styled to a similar design, it just isn't going to look the same.

With cavity-wall construction the inner leaf of the wall may allow you to house the new frames in a cavity closure after the inner leaf opening has been widened slightly. The use of proprietary insulated cavity closures

be cut through in the sequence shown in the diagram on page 57 and each part can be pulled away from the retained glass in the arrowed directions. The outer frame is the last thing to be cut through and prised away. The nails are likely to be rusty that take a frame fixing makes this possible; although these were designed for new-build, they work just as well here. You may only need an extra 50–70 mm on either side to achieve this, but the lintel should be checked first to ensure that end bearings of at least 150 mm are retained. By recessing the window behind the brick reveal you reduce the visible frame width and improve the appearance of the windows. Cills have to be cut to suit, and the lintel arrangement should be considered before you embark on this procedure, because it obviously isn't going to work in all situations. It helps if the outer face of brickwork is arched over the existing opening and the lintel is located behind it.

Solid-brick (225 mm/9 in) walls prevent you from recessing PVC-U frames, making purpose-made replacement timber frames the best choice in a period home. With any style of window, the frame should always be rebated (set back) at least 25 mm to the front face of the brickwork for weather resistance.

Given the availability of silicone mastic sealants and expanding foam, together with all those sections of PVC-U and a tube of super glue, finishing plastic windows is always possible. Even so, give yourself plenty of time to think of the best and most aesthetic solution before you set to, and remember that frame-fixing foam has now been recommended only in conjunction with mechanical fixings and shouldn't be used by itself to hold windows and doors in place.

In modern times timber frames have been able to accept vertical damp-proof courses (DPC) on their backs fixed with nails or staples, but plastic ones can't and new frames are often compromised in weather resistance because of this. Wind-blown rain can find a way through if silicone mastic is left as the sole defence against it. Window fitters don't like vertical DPCs, and when they find them on new-builds they tend to either cut them back flush with the wall closure or turn them inside out and fit the window frames on top of them, which means the plasterer will come along later and cut them off. What they don't seem to be able to do is trim and tuck them into the rebates on the back of the frame. Technology falls apart here in the hands of fitters and the DPC is viewed as superfluous, but quite often it does a vital job of keeping out the weather.

The most common problem with plastic windows is, however, in fixing them. Plastic bends and plastic frames will bend if over-enthusiastically fixed. You might think how nice it is to have a really solidly fixed window frame, up until the point when you fit the glass or the casements and find there are gaps around them because it is no longer square. Plastic window frames are easily pulled out of shape by frame fixings, or even by using timber-packing pieces instead of plastic. It's important that the windows are made to fit, but with a good 10 mm gap around the peripheries and with plastic wedge packers used in this gap near the fixings.

Replacing fascias and soffits

As if there isn't enough business in replacing windows and doors with plastic ones, the fascias and soffits of Britain are crying out never to be painted again. Now here is a renewal that is worth doing and doing well. I don't know anybody who enjoys redecorating the eaves of a house. This is ladder work of the worst kind – invariably the overhang is considerable and gives a wide soffit that you can't stand a ladder on beneath and still be able to repaint the fascia board. Ladders with stand-offs are needed.

Then there is the task of stripping the old paintwork, or at least sanding it down, before you can repaint. The temptation here to speed the job up is too much for some people, who have resorted to using a blowtorch to burn off the old paint. I can think of at least two cases locally in the last few years where this task has set fire to the roof, and in one case, burned down the neighbour's roof as well. While the blowtorch wielder was merrily working away outside, the timber was merrily smouldering from the heat inside and spread through the roof structure quietly by itself. Not until it was too late did the fire attract attention, and then the fire brigade's job was to save the house beneath the roof. What had started as a repainting job on the fascia turned out to be complete rebuilding of the roof structure. Ripping off the old timber fascia and soffit and replacing it with plastic will almost never involve the fire brigade.

When plastic fascias and soffits first came to the industry, window companies jumped on the idea as a

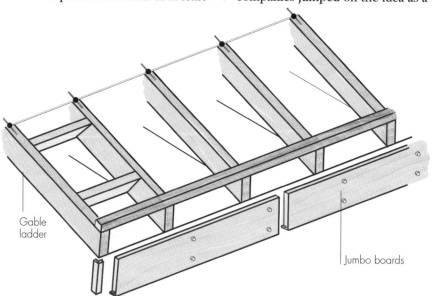

Remove old fascia before fitting new thick PVC-U fascia boards.

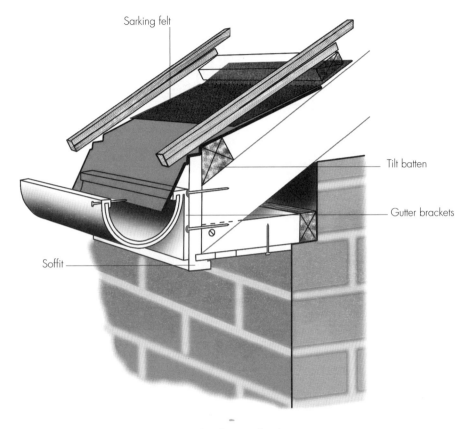

Sarking felt

Tilt batten

Gutter brackets

Soffit

Completed eaves detail.

sideline, but now the products are commonly available from merchants and stores so you can obtain it easily and smile about how inexpensive it is. The major cost involved in replacing fascias is the scaffold, followed by the labour. The materials are inexpensive, and are a joy to work with: cellular PVC is cut easily and cleanly with a saw, and comes protected by a film that you can peel back when you've finished. If it has a weakness, it can be scratched and damaged quite easily due to its softness.

Fascia boards come in a variety of sizes and thicknesses, but while it's common to get the right depth, not everybody gets the right thickness. With fascia you need enough strength to support the guttering, and this means buying thick material. Thicker products are around 16 mm, and thinner 6–10 mm. Plastic-headed nails with an annular shank to help them bite in are used for fixing, while the bodies of the nails are made from stainless steel to avoid any risk of corrosion over the years.

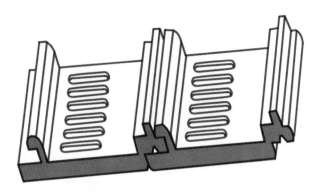

Interlocking soffit boards with pre-formed vents.

Of course, it makes the job a lot easier if you use the thinner stuff and nail it over the top of the existing boards, and much of the 'specialist' work sold in this area has been done this way. This will be fine for a while, but how long will depend on the condition of the timber beneath: partially encasing wood may not do it any good, and one day it will need to be removed. The only way to avoid future problems is to replace it with thick cellular board nailed direct to the rafter ends.

One other issue: in cavity walls where cavities exist unfilled by insulation, the top of the cavity is closed with a non-combustible product to prevent fire spread into the roof. This is connected to the blowtorch problem in that fire does enjoy creeping around in spaces where it can't be seen. To fire-stop the cavity at the eaves, builders have used cement-fibre-type boards, and to make the job even easier they've used soffit and widened to bridge the cavity. This

grey, brittle cement-fibreboard is just the stuff we like to replace with shiny white plastic. You can't even get paint to stick to cement-fibreboard, so replacing it is very popular.

Because plastic is combustible it can't be used as a fire barrier, so this will need to be replaced separately. Mineral fibre is the best answer. In cavity wall construction, mineral-fibre batts are used in walls. They are semi-rigid and can be cut into strips and stuffed in the head of the cavity. A 100–150 mm-deep strip should be sufficient and you may need to use oversized batts to get a sure fit (e.g. 65 mm thick batts for a 50 mm cavity). It may be possible to dress the roof insulation down over the wall plate to cover the cavity, but something that fits tightly to close it is best. Timber-frame houses bought as packaged kits come with cavity stops of mineral fibre sleeved in tubes of red polythene for this very purpose, and pinning these into place will make the job easier.

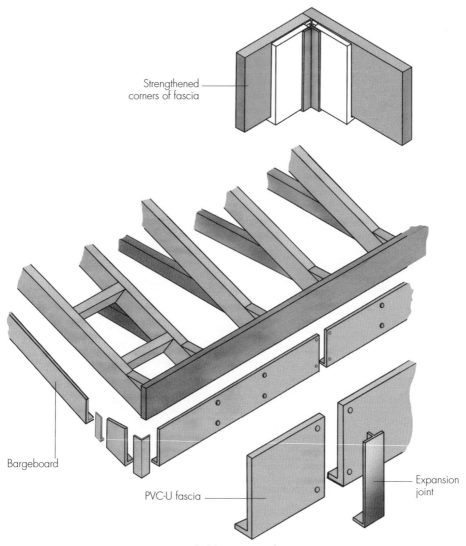

Strengthened corners of fascia

Bargeboard

PVC-U fascia

Expansion joint

Over-cladding existing fascias.

Plastic has one major flaw: it expands and contracts beneath the sun, and fascias and soffits can't be fitted tightly together without buckling. A 5 mm gap to each board end (making a 10 mm gap between boards) is needed, and this should be covered by jointing strips fixed with mastic silicone to accommodate the movement – they shouldn't be glued.

The gable verge's bargeboards can be a bit more of a problem than fascias and soffits, because in modern homes they are nailed to the part of the roof

63

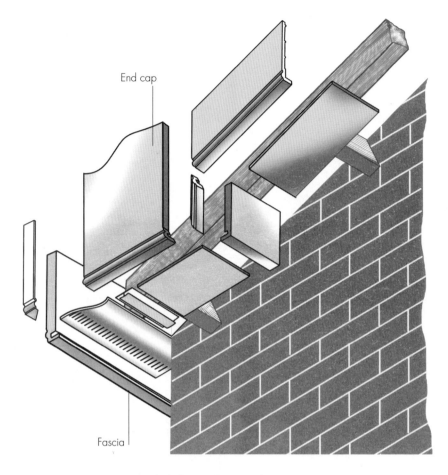

Exploded view of ogee-style components.

truss structure known as the gable ladder. The ladder is a bit of flimsy, 'loose-fixed' timber extended a bit over the cavity wall, and too much vigorous removal up here could do some damage – the verge tiles are likely to be mortar-bedded to an undercloak, and this will easily be loosened if not destroyed. If the verge undercloak has been formed with a cavity closing board as well, this will need the same treatment as the eaves. All things considered, you may want to overdress the bargeboard if the timber is still in good shape.

Chimneys and fireplaces

Before the 1950s the fireplace was the focal point in our homes. It might have changed in style and design as the decades and centuries went by, but it was always there as a place of warmth and security, and was something to look at. All that changed in the 1950s, when a smaller, box-like focal point was introduced to replace it, and ever since then we have preferred to watch it. Televisions were smaller then, and with their introduction, rooms became smaller and ceilings lower, and that is more or less where we are today with the home. However, fires have been enjoying a revival of late, not so much for heat and practical reasons as purely for aesthetic ones. Oh, and TVs are getting bigger – so isn't it about time we raised the ceilings back?

Fires, flues and carbon monoxide

Carbon monoxide, or CO[1] poisoning has been killing around 50 people every year. It's the worst kind of accidental death because it can easily be prevented. CO[1] is a gas, but it isn't only gas-fuelled appliances that can produce it; any fossil fuel can, and will do if the room is not properly ventilated or the appliance isn't working properly or, more commonly, if the flue is blocked or leaking. A combination of these factors can arise if the home hasn't been maintained. Vents get blocked off because of the unwanted draught, chimneys get sooted up and deposits fall down flues to the appliance below, gradually blocking it over time. If the appliance is used, soon the gas will start to leak into the room; silent and without smell, it goes unnoticed – until it's too late.

There are some signs to watch for. With gas fires, the flame is normally blue, but if it starts to burn yellow or orange, you have a problem. Switch it off and have it checked. Likewise, solid fuel fires may be awkward to light and slow to burn, and soot stains appear above the appliance, or even on it. The symptoms of poisoning are difficult to spot: you may experience tiredness, headaches, dizziness, feeling drowsy and nausea – in other words, flu-like symptoms – or you may just feel under the weather.

Chimneys and appliances need to be checked regularly by inspection and with tests to ensure they're safe for use.

Because of the risk of CO[1] poisoning while we sleep (and also because of central heating), fires are no longer used in bedrooms. If you do like the idea of installing a flame fire in one for a romantic atmosphere, make sure that it has a spillage safety device or a room-sealed balanced flue. Many of the decorative gas appliances that involve pebbles in place of coals have a low-rated output. Some at the bottom end of the rated output range (below 7kW) are sufficiently low to avoid combustion ventilation and spillage safety devices. Because guidance changes from time to time, and because you have the Gas Safety Regulations as well as the Building Regulations to comply with, check your appliances' requirements with both these controls before you design and install any fire.

Restoring old chimneys and fireplaces

Before you start work on renovating the fireplace or fitting a new appliance in it, you need to have the flue checked out. It isn't unusual for old brick chimneys to leak smoke, since they often have no flue lining. Even if you are planning to line the flue with a new flue-lining system, the existing flue will need to be swept first to remove all soot deposits. Oversized brick flues can be converted for use with a small appliance, such as a stove or gas fire. They may have to be lined with an appropriate flue system simply to reduce the size: flexible metal flue liners are commonly used to do this; although they may appear suited to any use, they have do limits – specifically, they are made with certain fuel types in mind, gas predominantly. Wood-burning stoves tend to produce tar-like deposits that make this type of fuel a fire risk.

It's good practice to replace old metal linings whenever you replace an appliance, unless you are very confident that they were recently installed and are suited to the new appliance you want to install.

Existing flues of any kind can become blocked by nests and debris, and just as easily as by soot and tar. Only by inspection and testing can any flue be re-commissioned into use.

A visual inspection is a good place to start, followed by a core-ball test on the flue. The main point of this test is to prove that the flue size is suited for the proposed use. A core ball is any heavy ball, sized to about 25 mm less than the flue diameter needed, fixed to a rope and lowered down the chimney. If a blockage is found, the rope can be tagged, pulled up and measured to locate the position of the blockage for removal later. Square flues should be tested with purpose-made square coring plates or blocks.

Alternatively, start by having the flue swept, which will remove minor obstructions and allow you to see the condition of the flue more easily. Take a good look at what comes down the chimney, to see if any bits of brick lining, for example, have been dislodged with the brush. Angled mirrors and lights can be used to see parts of the flue, and if you're replastering the chimney breasts in your renovation, the old plaster can be hacked off now to assess the brickwork. Look for holes and gaps as well as signs of tar or soot staining on the outside, which are signs of leaking. At this point a smoke test can be carried out to see whether there are any gaps or holes in the flue that will leak smoke into the home. Smoke-testing procedures are described as two types depending on the fuel proposed: type 1 tests for gas-tightness and is suitable for oil-fired or solid-fuel appliances, and type 2 tests are used where gas fires are to be fitted.

Type 1 smoke tests (oil or solid-fuel fires/appliances)

Resist the temptation to light the fire to test the chimney; smoke-testing pellets are much safer. You will need to close all the windows and doors to the room. The flue should be warmed up to create a draught by placing a portable electric radiator in or very near the fireplace opening. This might take ten minutes or more for large or cold chimneys, but it is necessary to ensure that an updraught is created for the smoke to rise up the chimney and not billow out into the room. Have a piece of board ready to support in place over the opening, or if a stove or burner is fitted with a door, close the door and seal off any vents or ash boxes with tape. In this test smoke has to go up, not out.

Ignite the smoke pellets and nip outside to wait for the smoke to appear from the chimney pots before sealing them off with a weighted-down board. Did I tell you a ladder is needed? Once both ends are sealed, you can inspect the chimney breasts throughout the home and look for signs of smoke wisping out. The test should stay on for at least five minutes, and you need to make sure that no smoke creeps out from any adjacent flues, which would indicate leakage between flues. Take your time to check the structure over – smoke has a habit of travelling through cavities like eaves overhangs and wall cavities, so it might emerge some distance from the chimney itself.

Type 2 smoke test (gas fires/appliances)

As described in type 1 tests, the flue should be warmed and the opening to the fireplace sealed off once the pellets have started to smoke. In this case, however, an air entry gap of around 25 mm should be left at the bottom of the board. There is no need to seal off the top of the chimney with this test – you only need to see the smoke appearing freely from the top and check the flue along its length to see that it doesn't appear anywhere else.

In both of these tests the occasional wisp of smoke appearing from the flue is acceptable and doesn't necessarily fail the test. However, significant quantities of smoke will. The reason for this is because smoke pellets generate smoke at much higher pressure than the flue would normally experience in working mode.

Air and vents

Apart from making sure the combustion of an appliance works correctly by providing it with enough oxygen, air also helps to ensure that combustion gases find their way out through the flue, and in some situations it keeps the appliance casing cool enough to touch. The actual amount of air you need depends on the fuel you are burning and the rated ouput of the appliance.

With solid-fuel or oil-burning stoves, the vent area needed increases with the rated output of the appliance and with the presence of a draught break.

Open-flued boilers that you wish to hide in a cupboard can usually be ventilated through the door into the room, if that room itself has permanent ventilation. It does mean that the cupboard doors may have to be louvred to let in enough air, since the need is greater when drawing the air from an adjoining space than direct from the outside.

Otherwise, traditional air bricks can be chopped into the outside walls. They have a given free vent area to compare to the vent area required. The makers of these products produce this information, so you don't have to measure the holes!

Fires without flues and vents

At this stage I should mention the new age of technology. The latest fires are environmentally friendly, clean-burning devices that don't give off smoke at all. And to cap it all they don't rely on drawn in air to burn; instead they use 'secondary air', which ignites the smoke when pre-heated. In this way they heat up the air to the temperature of the fire chamber and then inject it over the fuel in the fire bed, setting alight to the smoke before it even thinks about going up the chimney, thus completely changing the saying about things going up in smoke and modifying the one about 'no smoke without fire'. These new devices have the rare ability to keep a flame fire alive when in fact it should be doing no more than smouldering.

Giving this piece of technological art, fireplace makers have been busy creating frames of glass and stainless steel for hole-in-the-wall fires. Our fashion at the moment seems to reside here with these minimalist looks of clean, stark, smooth materials that look bright and polished.

Fires have always been fashion accessories, and the style that is in today may not be in tomorrow. Technology has brought them to a place now where they have never been before. Not so many years ago 'flame-effect' electric fires created a poor illusion of a real fire involving a lamp and a revolving blind. Flame-effect today means actual flame – but one that can be ignited and adjusted by a wireless remote control from the comfort of your armchair.

Until very recently any non-electric fire, whether gas, oil or solid-fuel, needed a flue – a pipe from which the exhaust gases could escape out of the building. But now with catalytic technology, gas fires without flues can be installed to give you total freedom on where you position them. By 2003, some 50 million homes worldwide had them installed, and in Japan these appliances have been outselling conventional flued fires by 15 to 1. Britain certainly has some catching up to do.

Flueless fires work safely by drawing in combustion air from the room at the base of the appliance, but also by introducing air through a heat exchanger wrapped around the back of the combustion chamber. Heat exchangers are energy-efficiency devices, and without a flue for some heat to be wasted into, 100 per cent of the heat is used. Running costs are said to be about a third of those of conventional, flued gas fires, which makes them just about perfect in energy-efficiency terms.

Energy efficiency is great, but what really makes these appliances desirable is the freedom to install them anywhere: internal walls, room dividers, wherever you have the space, without having to look for an external wall from which you can install a flue.

Fireplace surrounds

Even without a chimney the fireplace surround has become a popular feature once again, and a good deal of design work has gone into the choice of materials and styles available. Some of the materials used in decorative surrounds are extremely heavy, and you will need to choose a method of fixing them to the wall that is safe and secure. Marble surrounds have been known to come away, and in one

tragic accident one seriously injured a three-year-old child. Fitted by a specialist company using a gypsum-based adhesive that was not suited to this kind of weight, and without any kind of mechanical fixings, the surround was destined to eventually come away from the wall, which it did at the wrong time. Make sure your installers use mechanical fixings like screws or expansion bolts in addition to adhesive.

Original fireplaces in period homes are top of the list for renovation. They may be suffering from chips and

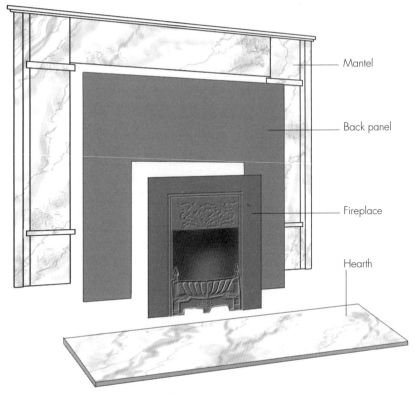

Mantel

Back panel

Fireplace

Hearth

Fireplace components.

Tiled fireplace surround.

cracks, missing pieces or just general discolouration. Some may have been painted over rather badly. Metal or stone surrounds such as marble can be stripped of old paintwork with paint removers, although stained marble can be cleaned with specialist materials. A poultice of fuller's earth and talc mixed with clean water can work effectively, combined of course with lashings of elbow grease.

Ceramic tiles were used by the Victorians to surround fireplaces, but in fact the idea dates further back to the Georgians, who favoured Delftware tiles for this purpose.

Building a new chimney

Brick chimneys are structures that require plenty of attention to design and detail if they are to be problem-free. Perhaps because we haven't been building new homes with chimneys for some time, much of the skills and knowledge has been lost, and some chimneys are prone to smoking or damp penetration soon after they've been constructed.

Structure

Chimneys are structures of considerable weight that need to be supported, which means that they

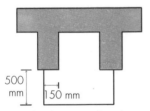

500 mm | 150 mm

Fireplace: minimum hearth size

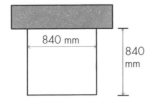

840 mm

840 mm

Freestanding fire: minimum hearth size

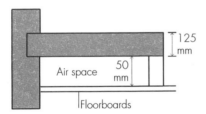

125 mm

Air space | 50 mm

Floorboards

Superimposed hearth over timber floor

Critical minimum hearth dimensions.

shouldn't be built up from floors but formed on suitable foundations in the subsoil beneath.

It's a depressing thought, but an internal chimney means a hole in the floor to start with. External chimneys built on external walls may have their foundations dug outside your home as if they were small extensions. Chimney foundations are usually just pads of concrete that will spread the load into the subsoil, and like any foundation, that means having some awareness of

what both those figures are. Brickwork has a mass of around 19 kg/cu m, which can be multiplied to the volume of the chimney to get a total weight. Subsoil comes in a variety of types with a given bearing pressure that is only specific to itself, so inspections have to be made of the excavation before it is concreted. You can assume a safe bearing load in the subsoil but it pays to make modest assumptions and err on the side of caution.

Large, inglenook-style brick chimneys attached to modern homes are best formed in cavity construction at the bottom (as far as the breasts extend up the outside wall) before being reduced to single brick for the chimney itself above roof level. Bricks and mortar aren't waterproof, and the cavity will serve at this level to stop driving rain from getting through to the inside. Smaller chimneys that merely enclose the flue could be single-brick throughout. Either type needs to penetrate the roof level and continue up enough to safely disperse the smoke. The dimensions for this 'enough' change with regulations and codes from time to time, and you will need to check the current version, but a height above ridge of at least 600 mm is essential and at least 1800 mm above the roof slope. With steeply pitched roofs you will also need to be aware of the distance from the pots to the slope (measured horizontally), and this can have a bearing on the feasibility of the project, so check the current standards sooner than later.

Slenderness is another factor with chimneys. To stop them swaying in the

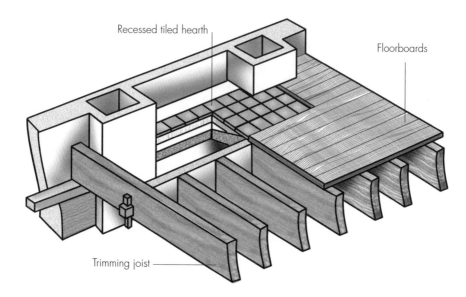

Recessed tiled hearth

Floorboards

Trimming joist

Recessed hearth.

breeze they can't be too tall for their width. Four and half times is a guide limit if you don't want to have to build in a metal tie bar to restrain the stack.

Damp
New chimneys suffered in the wet winter of 2001. Many people had been building them with pretty but soft facing bricks that allowed the rain to soak through to the flue itself, from where it ran down the flue face and appeared in the room below. Damp-proof courses built into chimneys do a sound job, but they need to be taken to the flue itself, and it is wise to join them with a flue joint. So long as the joint can still be formed (these joints are usually socket and spigot joints) and it doesn't leak smoke, this will be enough.

Flues
Traditionally a minimum 200 mm square or diameter flue is enough for an open fire, but this works with regular-size fireplace openings of up to 500 x 550 mm. Inglenooks and bigger openings will always pose a problem. A larger size fire opening, or a centre fireplace design that is open on two sides, warrants a larger flue that is 15 per cent of the opening size in its cross-sectional area. Look out for the availability of liners in this situation, as it really isn't acceptable these days to build new chimneys unlined. You can install a flue liner that will serve a gas-effect fire, such as one of the real-flame-effect types controlled from your armchair remote, but it is likely to restrict your choice of fire in the future.

Building a new chimney is costly, and if you are planning on spending that much money, you might as well build in a flue for a real fire. It will mean that it can be converted in later life if you decide to fit a stove or some other appliance. Constructing it so that it can only be used with a decorative gas fire will prevent it being upgraded to an open fire later.

Certificates

If you have employed a professional to conduct any inspection or testing of your fireplace, flue, chimney or hearth, you should ensure that you receive a certificate from them. The details should include the address and a full description of the construction of the chimney, flue hearth and type of appliance, ventilation provision, flue terminal details etc, as well as the tests carried out and the results. The certificate should declare the name and qualifications of the person testing and their registration number. Suitable registration bodies include:

HETAS – Solid-fuel appliance engineers
CORGI – Gas-appliance engineers
OFTEC – Oil-appliance engineers
NACE – Chimney engineers
NACS – Chimney sweeps

Registration bodies structure their member's qualifications to different specialities, so do not be afraid to check the registration details of individuals. They might hold registration cards with photo IDs, but they may be qualified only to carry out pipework or installations, not inspections or testing.

CHAPTER FOUR

Rewiring and Lighting

Existing wiring

One day, I have no doubt, an Electrical Inspection Report on a home's wiring will have to accompany every conveyance. But in 2004, as before, the words of the estate agent's blurb, 'Not inspected', will continue to fall sadly short of being useful, and homes will continue to be sold without an electrician's certificate of inspection and testing endorsing the electrical system. One step at a time, though: perhaps in the near future, if a certificate isn't available buyers will be able to assume that remedial work is needed to bring it into compliance, and they can then decide whether or not to go ahead with the purchase.

If you're a landlord renting out your property, or a hotelier, for example, such certificates have been needed for some time, but traditionally homes have always been sold without any comment on the safety of the electrics. Many a pair of pliers have been welded together by unexpectedly live cables, and cases of earth leakage have resulted in electrified walls or a kitchen sink becoming live and lethal. Our workplaces are meant to have their circuits tested every five years by a registered electrician, and every ten years is recommended for homes, but how many of us have actually followed that advice?

Checking out existing electrics

There is no substitute for using a qualified electrician to inspect and test the system, but you can start the process by looking at the general condition and making notes yourself. Begin with the meter cupboard and the consumer unit. To help you, a checklist is given below, and the results should help you form a view of the system and its health in general. You can tell a good deal about the state of the circuits simply by looking. The checklist will enable you to assess the general condition of the installation, but you will need the services of a qualified electrician to fully test and inspect it.

Visual inspection checklist
Fuseboard and meter
GENERAL CONDITION

● Is the equipment fixed securely to the wall?

● Is the equipment dry?

● Are any parts of it broken or damaged?

Fuses (fuseboard) with the power switched off

● Are the fuseholders and fuses intact, complete and not broken?

● Are the correct fuses fitted? Before the advent of MCBs in the 1980s, fuses were fitted to colour-coded holders of a unique size for their current rating: 30 amp red, 5 amp blue, etc.

Cables
- Do they appear to be in good condition and undamaged?

- Do they appear to be connected? Check that none are loose or hanging free.

Fuseboard
- Is there a list of circuits within the fuseboard (perhaps inside the cover), and if so, is it complete? Are the fuses to the circuits identified?

Circuits
GENERAL
- Are cables clipped to walls, floor and ceiling joists in attics and the voids beneath floorboards?

- Is wiring safely located away from accidental damage and children?

- Has a residual current device been fitted to any external supply or in general at the fuseboard?

Lighting
- Do all the lights work?

- Are the ceiling pendent flexes above the lamp-holders in good condition and not scorched or frayed?

- With the ceiling roses and lamp holders unscrewed, are the wires all connected and sheathed with insulation (no bare wires)?

- Are the switches, lamp-holders and ceiling roses complete and

undamaged?. Even those used in the 1970s may now be brittle and easily cracked.

- Are the switches fixed properly, and do they operate positively?

Power sockets
- Do they all work correctly?

- Do they all have switches?

- Are they fixed securely to the wall?

- Are they in good condition with no evidence of scorching or discolouration?

- Do they grip the plugs firmly?

- Are there sufficient numbers of outlets in rooms?

Cooker points and water heaters
- Are any retained appliances correctly wired with the right size of cable? Are the cables rated for current?

- Do the control switches work correctly?

- Are they firmly fixed to the wall?

- Are they complete and undamaged?

Inspection reports
To formalise this list you will need to commission a qualified and registered electrician who is able to issue a Periodic Inspection Report with reference to BS:7671 (IEE Wiring

HOME RENOVATIONS

Form 6

Form No   /6

PERIODIC INSPECTION REPORT FOR AN ELECTRICAL INSTALLATION (note 1)
(REQUIREMENTS FOR ELECTRICAL INSTALLATIONS - BS 7671 [IEE WIRING REGULATIONS])

DETAILS OF THE CLIENT

Client: ....

Address: ....

Purpose for which this Report is required: .... (note 3)

DETAILS OF THE INSTALLATION Tick boxes as appropriate

Occupier: ....

Installation: ....

Address: ....

Description of Premises: Domestic ☐   Commercial ☐   Industrial ☐   Other ☐

....

Estimated age of the Electrical   .... years
Installation:

Evidence of Alterations or Additions: Yes ☐   No ☐   Not apparent ☐

If "Yes", estimate age: .... years

Date of last inspection: ....   Records available   Yes ☐   No ☐

EXTENT AND LIMITATIONS OF THE INSPECTION (note 5)

Extent of electrical installation covered by this report: ....

....

....

Limitations: ....

....

....

This inspection has been carried out in accordance with BS 7671 : 2001 (IEE Wiring Regulations), amended to ....
Cables concealed within trunking and conduits, or cables and conduits concealed under floors, in roof spaces and
generally within the fabric of the building or underground have not been inspected.

NEXT INSPECTION (note 8)

I/We recommend that this installation is further inspected and tested after an interval of not more than .... months/years,
provided that any observations 'requiring urgent attention' are attended to without delay.

DECLARATION

INSPECTED AND TESTED BY

Name: ....   Signature: ....

For and on behalf of: ....   Position: ....

Address: ....

....   Date: ....

....

Page 1 of

SUPPLY CHARACTERISTICS AND EARTHING ARRANGEMENTS Tick boxes and enter details, as appropriate

Earthing arrangements	Number and Type of Live Conductors	Nature of Supply Parameters	Supply Protective Device Characteristics
TN-C ☐ TN-S ☐ TN-C-S ☐ TT ☐ IT ☐	a.c. ☐ d.c. ☐ 1-phase, 2-wire ☐ 2-pole ☐ 1-phase, 3 wire ☐ 3-pole ☐	Nominal voltage, U/U_o [(1)] .... V Nominal frequency, f [(1)] .... Hz Prospective fault current, I_{pf} [(2)] .... kA (note 4) External loop impedance, Z_e [(2)] .... Ω	Type:................... .... Nominal current rating ....A
Alternative source ☐ of supply (to be detailed on attached schedules)	2-phase, 3-wire ☐ other ☐ 3-phase, 3-wire ☐ 3-phase, 4-wire ☐	(Note: (1) by enquiry, (2) by enquiry or by measurement)	

PARTICULARS OF INSTALLATION REFERRED TO IN THE REPORT Tick boxes and enter details, as appropriate

Means of Earthing
Supplier's facility ☐
Installation earth electrode ☐

Details of Installation Earth Electrode (*where applicable*)

Type (e.g. rod(s), tape etc)	Location	Electrode resistance to earth
....	....	.... Ω

Main Protective Conductors

Earthing conductor: material .... csa ....mm²   connection verified ☐
Main equipotential bonding conductors   material .... csa ....mm²   connection verified ☐

To incoming water service ☐   To incoming gas service ☐   To incoming oil service ☐   To structural steel ☐
To lightning protection ☐   To other incoming service(s) ☐   (state details..)

Main Switch or Circuit-breaker

BS, Type.. No. of poles ....   Current rating ....A   Voltage rating V

Location..   Fuse rating or setting ....A

Rated residual operating current $I_{\Delta n}$ = ... mA, and operating time of .... ms (at $I_{\Delta n}$) (applicable only where an RCD is suitable and is used as a main circuit-breaker)

OBSERVATIONS AND RECOMMENDATIONS Tick boxes as appropriate
(note 9)

Recommendations as detailed below

Referring to the attached Schedule(s) of Inspection and Test Results, and subject to the limitations specified at the Extent and Limitations of the Inspection section

note 6

☐ No remedial work is required   ☐ The following observations are made:

....
....
....
....
....
....

One of the following numbers, as appropriate, is to be allocated to each of the observations made above to indicate to the person(s) responsible for the installation the action recommended.

| 1 | requires urgent attention | 2 | requires improvement | 3 | requires further investigation |

| 4 | does not comply with BS 7671: 2001 amended to .... This does not imply that the electrical installation inspected is unsafe.

SUMMARY OF THE INSPECTION (note 7)

Date(s) of the inspection: ....
General condition of the installation: ....
....
....

Overall assessment: Satisfactory/Unsatisfactory (note 8)

SCHEDULE(S)
The attached Schedules are part of this document and this Report is valid only when they are attached to it.
.... Schedule(s) of Inspections and .... Schedule(s) of Test Results are attached.
(Enter quantities of schedules attached).

Regulations); an example of which is shown on page 76. It has been designed for checking existing installations only, not for carrying out new work. The purpose of the report should be stated on it. This could be to ascertain compliance with the current wiring regulations, or perhaps to simply report on the safety condition of the cabling and equipment. Make sure you agree with your electrician what the purpose is and check that it's stated on the forms.

The extent and any limitations of the report should also be clearly stated, although these should not appear in the form of a surprise – your contractor should have made you aware beforehand.

Reports are normally formed in sections and include the test results on the circuits, earthing arrangements and circuit breakers. Observations and recommendations are detailed and awarded ratings of priority for action.

FOUR RATINGS FOR PRIORITISING ACTION

1 Requires urgent attention

2 Requires improvement

3 Requires further investigation

4 Does not comply with IEE Wiring Regulations (current edition), but this does not mean the installation is unsafe for use

Rewiring, testing and certification

Registered electricians and DIY

The recognised bodies for electricians are the NICEIC (National Inspection Council for Electrical Installation Contracting) and the ECA (Electrical Contractors Association), and you should look for a contractor that is registered with either. In employing them, a certificate of testing and compliance with the relevant standards of safety and quality will be available to you for any work they do. This is particularly beneficial when it's notifiable work under the Building Regulations: this could mean adding extra power sockets or light points, and only a suitably qualified (i.e. registered with the NICEIC or the ECA) electrician will be able to self-certify the work and avoid a Building Control Service application.

If you plan to do the work yourself or use an unregistered electrician, it will certainly pay to have it inspected and tested by a qualified electrician once you've finished. Two different certificates are available: one is for complete rewired (new) circuits, and the other is for minor electrical work like alterations.

Rewired (new) circuits

The job of rewiring a complete circuit is best carried out by a registered electrician who can cover his work by an Electrical Installation Certificate (see opposite). This certificate is meant for new work that has been designed, constructed, inspected and tested in accordance with BS:7671. If one person is responsible for all four of these, he has the honour of signing in that capacity. If four separate individuals are responsible for the different parts, the name, address and

ELECTRICAL INSTALLATION CERTIFICATE (notes 1 and 2)
(REQUIREMENTS FOR ELECTRICAL INSTALLATIONS - BS 7671 [IEE WIRING REGULATIONS])

DETAILS OF THE CLIENT (note 1) ....
....
....

INSTALLATION ADDRESS ....
....
.... Postcode ....

DESCRIPTION AND EXTENT OF THE INSTALLATION Tick boxes as appropriate
(note 1)

Description of installation: ....

Extent of installation covered by this Certificate:
....
....
....
....

New installation	☐
Addition to an existing installation	☐
Alteration to an existing installation	☐

FOR DESIGN

I/We being the person(s) responsible for the design of the electrical installation (as indicated by my/our signatures below), particulars of which are described above, having exercised reasonable skill and care when carrying out the design hereby CERTIFY that the design work for which I/we have been responsible is to the best of my/our knowledge and belief in accordance with BS 7671 : ...., amended to ....(date) except for the departures, if any, detailed as follows:

> Details of departures from BS 7671 (Regulations 120-01-03, 120-02):

The extent of liability of the signatory or the signatories is limited to the work described above as the subject of this Certificate.

For the DESIGN of the installation: **(Where there is mutual responsibility for the design)

Signature: .... Date:........................... Name (BLOCK LETTERS):... Designer No 1

Signature:.............................. Date:........................... Name (BLOCK LETTERS):... Designer No 2**

FOR CONSTRUCTION

I/We being the person(s) responsible for the construction of the electrical installation (as indicated by my/our signatures below), particulars of which are described above, having exercised reasonable skill and care when carrying out the construction hereby CERTIFY that the construction work for which I/we have been responsible is to the best of my/our knowledge and belief in accordance with BS 7671 : ...., amended to ....(date) except for the departures, if any, detailed as follows:

> Details of departures from BS 7671 (Regulations 120-01-03, 120-02):

The extent of liability of the signatory is limited to the work described above as the subject of this Certificate.

For CONSTRUCTION of the installation:

Signature .... Date..

Name (BLOCK LETTERS) .... Constructor

FOR INSPECTION & TESTING

I/We being the person(s) responsible for the inspection & testing of the electrical installation (as indicated by my/our signatures below), particulars of which are described above, having exercised reasonable skill and care when carrying out the inspection & testing hereby CERTIFY that the work for which I/we have been responsible is to the best of my/our knowledge and belief in accordance with BS 7671 : ...., amended to ....(date) except for the departures, if any, detailed as follows:

> Details of departures from BS 7671 (Regulations 120-01-03, 120-02):

The extent of liability of the signatory is limited to the work described above as the subject of this Certificate.

For INSPECTION AND TEST of the installation:

Signature .... Date..

Name (BLOCK LETTERS) .... Inspector

NEXT INSPECTION (notes 4 and 7)

I/We the designer(s), recommend that this installation is further inspected and tested after an interval of not more than .... years/months.

signature afforded of each person must be included on the certificate. It doesn't have to be a complete rewire of the entire home; different forms allow for alterations or additions to existing circuits too, and each of these should be accompanied by a schedule of inspection and testing.

Alterations and checks

A Minor Electrical Installation Works Certificate should be awarded to any 'add-on' bits to the existing circuit, but not where a whole new circuit is constructed. For example, adding an extra socket outlet to an existing ring-main circuit would be covered by a Minor Electrical Installation Works Certificate. Although adding a plug-point seems like a minor task, there are still five basic tests that are considered essential:

● Check that the earth contact of the socket outlet is properly connected to the main earthing terminal.

● Measure the earth fault loop impedance and check that the maximum permitted disconnection time is not exceeded.

● Measure the extended circuit's insulation resistance and check that it complies with BS:7671 requirements.

● Check that the polarity of the socket-outlet is correct.

● Check that the RCD (if there is one) works to protect the circuit.

Some of these tests require the use of a test meter, and simple versions, available from DIY stores, are able to carry out these tasks perfectly well.

Installing and sizing new cables

Circuits need ratings and calculations of the load (power output) from the appliances on them to establish what type of cable is required. Cables are rated by the thickness of the copper wire inside and its resistance, but also by the fact that they may be partially buried in insulation, where they run through a roof void for instance. Because this can be a cause of overheating, they have to be downrated to compensate.

Lighting circuits are commonly in 1–1.5 mm twin and earth cable, depending on the length and load to the circuit (1.5 mm sq cable will add about 50 per cent to the maximum length of the circuit) and ring mains are 2.5 mm sq. Apart from the ring main circuits looping around your home, you may also have dead-ended circuits known as radial circuits spurred off them to pick up remote places, but wherever they run off to, they end there.

Lighting circuits are generally extended to cover no more than about eight lights, if there is any uncertainty over the wattage of the lamps that are going to be fitted. This number could be significantly increased if lamps of no more than 100W, for example, were to be assumed. In the past our circuits were connected together by junction boxes, and many older homes are riddled with hidden boxes in the floor and roof voids. Since the early 1980s it has been common to use loop-in circuits instead. These use the ceiling roses instead of a junction box by picking up each light fitting as they go around the circuit, with four terminals in each fitting (including the earth terminal), allowing wires to run in from the switching as well as supply the powering and loop-in to the next fitting on the circuit.

New cables need to be safely routed through your home and clipped at regular intervals to joists and wall surfaces, using the correct size clips. Surface wiring must be tempting in any rewiring project, but it should be avoided at every opportunity. To use surface-mounted switch and socket boxes on walls is one thing, but using surface-mounted wires run inside plastic conduits is another. Decoratively it looks disastrous and cheap.

Cables are normally run out of sight inside floor and roof voids. On walls they should be housed in protective metal conduits and buried beneath the plaster. This means cutting out a shallow channel in the wall, using special tools to do this neatly and expediently. Some replastering is inevitable, and you should give this some thought when deciding where the switches and outlets are to go. Cables can be run inside timber stud walls but not inside the cavities of masonry cavity walls. Wherever they are hidden, straight lines are required between the fittings so that home owners of the future can predict where they are before they drill holes or nail in fittings.

You can see from the table below that the cable you need is dependent on de-rating factors. When cables are surrounded by insulation, overheating risks are increased and the amount of current that the cable is able to carry is significantly reduced.

En-suite and bathroom wiring
Earth bonding
Correct earth bonding is an essential element of electrical safety, and tests can be conducted to determine its continuity. In the majority of homes, the earthing arrangement stems from the main earthing bar in the consumer unit. Only earth wires acting as the

DE-RATED CABLE CAPACITIES			
Cable size	6 mm sq	10 mm sq	16 mm sq
Inside an insulated wall	32 amp	43 amp	57 amp
Inside conduit/trunking	38 amp	52 amp	69 amp
Inside a non-insulated wall clipped to a structure	46 amp	63 amp	85 amp

main equipotential bonding may run to metal water and gas service pipes, often at the point of the supply entry. The thickness of these wires was increased in the 1980s. It has not been permitted for installation earthing to be connected to these pipes since 1966, prior to which water pipes were used.

While all the circuits will have earth wires connecting back to the main bar, special zones like bathrooms should have extra bonding attached to water pipes, metal heating pipes, metal baths and basins and other exposed conductive parts. The combination of water and electricity is a lethal one, and the opportunity for electricity to short out through metal pipework and await the touch of wet hands is a dangerous one.

Special zones such as these attract more onerous requirements for wiring because of the increased risk. All exposed metal parts, such as metal baths, radiators and pipes, must be earth-bonded together using a sufficiently sized cable. The current edition of the IEE Wiring Regulations gives full details of what size cable and what bonding measures are required.

Electric showers

The electricity supply for most electric showers cannot be taken from the ring main. With ring mains running at 30 amps and lighting circuits at 15 amps, they are inadequately rated. Showers tend to require 45-amp circuits, and that means a separate circuit back to the consumer unit. Before you go ahead with your shower installation project, check that the

consumer unit has a spare fuseway that can provide this. If it doesn't, this will mean adding another unit or replacing the existing one with something larger.

When choosing the cable size for wiring an electric shower, the current-carrying capacity achieved must be at least equal to that of the shower rating. For example, a 45-amp rating from a 10.5 kW shower, with the cable buried in an insulated wall, will require a 16 mm sq cable achieving a capacity of 57 amps. A 10 mm sq cable in this instance would only achieve a 43-amp capacity. Another potential problem is if the cable has to run a long way back to the consumer unit; chances are that it will be encased in insulation somewhere, and it is best to use a 10 mm sq cable to cover this and stay safe. It's worth mentioning that if several cables are bundled together, the same effect as being encased by insulation can be produced and de-rating factors should be used.

A 45-amp double pole switch should be included in the circuit to isolate the supply when necessary. This switch needs to be placed above the outside of the bathroom door opening, so that it isn't used by mistake or with wet hands. If you'd rather not do this, your only other choice is a pull-cord ceiling-mounted switch which can go inside the room – either way, the switch should have a neon indicator to reveal whether the supply is on or off. Remember that it should be impossible to touch the switch body while standing in the bath or shower.

If shower installation is in the bedroom and not in a separate en-suite or bathroom, it is essential that all the socket outlets in the bedroom are protected by a 30 mA residual current device (RCD).

Intelligent home systems

You can take rewiring one step further, or rather in terms of the amount of cabling needed one leap further, by installing an intelligent system. Here, computer-controlled circuits replace or override manual switching of lights and appliances with more advanced controls. I don't just mean timers; computers have the benefit of being addressable by e-mail, phone or even text messaging, all of which can be used to contact your home and switch things on or off. Not only that, but with the use of computers to do the switching, a lot of basic and extra services in your home can be used without you being there – such as switching on heating and lighting, and even drawing the curtains or running a bath.

To date I've only seen an intelligent system installed in multi-million-pound renovations as an overstated toy that controls the plasma TV and ceiling-speakered hi-fi, so it's been somewhat gimmicky – gadgets for the luxury home or bachelor pad. The idea could take off on a more practical level: for example, the improved security from controlling the lighting or the curtains when you're away must be a real benefit. The motorised curtain track has limitations, though; as a miniature version of an electric garage door it

works well if all you have is standard drape curtains (although I know I'd worry about the motor burning out and setting fire to the curtains while on was on holiday), but for those who want voiles or Roman blinds – or anything other than drapes – they don't seem to be practical.

An intelligent system that lets you control your lighting or heating system by remote control is more likely to be popular, but absolutely top of the list for me is the central locking system that locks or unlocks all of the doors remotely and sets the burglar alarm. No more counting to ten seconds as you rush the family through the front door. You just sit in the car on the drive and press the remote key, much the same as you did to unlock the car. I don't know why the technology has been there for cars but not for homes, but it is on its way – heading up the garden path, so to speak, if not actually at the front door by now.

The key (excuse the pun) to the reliability of central locking is the fact that it uses no external cylinders. Cylinders on locks are vulnerable to attack from burglars. The state-of-the art remote central locking system uses high-security digital communication in encrypted transmissions, millions of combinations and the ability to disable the system if a key is lost, and the system can be wired in with smoke alarms to automatically release escape window and door locks when the alarms are triggered.

Commercial properties have used technology in fire safety like this for many years. It won't do away with you losing the keys that are still exactly where you put them down, but it will do away with doors or windows being accidentally left open. You can contact your home via cellphone to receive an update on the security status, and you could even open a door remotely to let in a neighbour to feed the cat. There is the possibility of wireless systems that use radio signals connecting to electronic controls fitted to locks. Where these systems could really take off is in the replacement window and door market.

You need an IT engineer or an electrician with experience in this area and a methodical mind to wire it. The colour-coded cabling that goes with an intelligent system does so in arm-thickness bundles. In extraordinary cases I've seen builders having to use air bricks or drain pipes as sleeves built into walls between rooms to pass the bundled cables through. If you have to pass cables through the joists, rather than between them, be aware if you reach this extreme of the hole drilling limits of floor joists, as exceeding these limits can weaken the floor structure of your home.

Intelligent house systems are here to stay in some form or another, but I tend to think it will be on a much reduced scale and restricted to the practical things that we want from our homes, and not the gimmicks. Starter wiring kits are available fairly cheaply from electrical merchants and DIY stores if you want to begin the process now. Even if you don't, you can build in the infrastructure for a future system now while you're renovating and save yourself a lot of work one day.

Future-proofing your home with ducts does make sense when you've got the floors up or new partitions being built. All it takes is some plastic pipe clipped inside the structure and terminated in wall boxes that are covered for now. So if you can build in some polythene duct pipe, do so. It will make feeding cables through so much easier later on. Ductwork, such as that used for mains water, gas and electric, is ideal, but remember that the service industry has colour codes for its supply services, so don't use a colour that will cause confusion one day: water pipe is blue, gas pipe yellow, electric is black, and fibre-optic communication cables are green. White might be a safe bet, and you might wish to use the external electric conduit system that comes with bends and fittings.

Electric heating

It may be the cleanest fuel, but we have been moving away from electric heating since the 1970s. The radiators were expensive to run, and the plugged-in look said 'council flat' rather than 'executive home' for too many people. Today's electric radiators have improved, with slimline storage types and roomstat controls as well as programmable thermostatic radiator controls that can be fitted to each and every radiator.

There is an alternative. Electric underfloor heating has reappeared to compete with the self-builder's

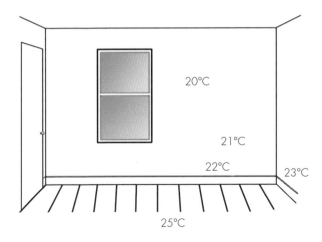

Heat radiation from a floor heating system

favourite of underfloor hot-water heating, which has metres of plastic tubing laid on insulation trays that need to be buried in floor screed, laborious work that is unsuited to renovations unless you happen to be rebuilding the ground floor slab.

Electric systems, on the other hand, can be laid within the finishings and are perfect for home renovations. They consist of thin matting that can be unrolled and tiled or boarded over, making them ideal for replacement floor-finishing jobs. Take the kitchen floor, for example: you've decided to tile it but you hate the idea of it being

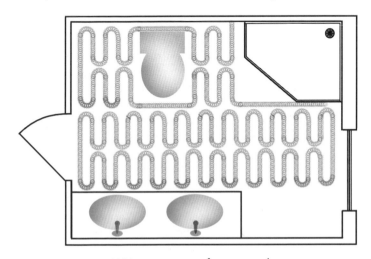

Wiring systems can fit any room layout.

cold to walk on. With the old floor finish removed and the surface cleaned, the heating matt of fine mesh with heating cables attached can be laid and primed over. The primer is only a few millimetres thick but provides a level base to tile to. With wall-hung radiators you basically have to live with a hot panel cooking at around 65°C in one small area of wall and a variety of air temperatures around the room, depending on the distance from it. Heated floors can have an even surface temperature of 25°C. giving a uniform 20–21°C to the air throughout the volume of the room.

As well as kitchens, bathroom floors can also be electrically heated, so when you step out of the shower it needn't be on to a cold tiled floor. A solid concrete floor structure isn't necessary, as electric systems can be overlaid on timber floors and covered by tiling, laminate or any other floating finishes. The heating cable used in these systems can be self-regulating in terms of the amount of heat output. In cold areas it releases more and in warm areas less, which means that if you have rugs or sunlit areas it won't overheat the floor, and where cold draughts or chilly spots exist it will compensate. Heat outputs range from 35–100W or more per square metre.

As with any heating system, roomstats can control the heat output as well, and some with integrated timers can bring the heating on at particular times. This is critical with underfloor heating, because it takes much longer to heat a room from a cold start than conventional radiators do. Some timers can predict warm-up time and are known as optimum start controls. They calculate how long it will take to heat the room to the required temperature at a required time of day and bring the heating on at just the right time needed to achieve this. Floor-level thermostats are also used in these systems to compare the two temperatures and achieve those optimum start times.

How much heat output you require from your electric floor heating will depend partly on how much insulation you have in your home. Ground floors without any insulation will need the 100W per square metre end of the ratings, while well-insulated homes can find 50W per square metre more than enough. The calculation needed to determine your heating requirements is no different than that for conventional radiators. The rate at which the room loses its heat is used to see how much heat is needed to maintain the comfortable temperature.

The heat loss is essentially a calculation of the area of the elements (external walls, floors and roofs), which is then multiplied by the U-value for that element. U-values are figures given to the thermal transmittance of an element, such as a wall. They can be precisely calculated if all the materials and construction of the element are known, but with existing homes the best you may be able to do is approximate them. The sum is the total heat loss from the room, so you have to design in heating to compensate for that heat loss. A

ROUGH GUIDE TO U-VALUES

EXTERNAL WALLS

Solid wall	1.60
Pre-1965 cavity wall	1.00
Built 1965–84	0.75
Built 1985–90	0.60
Built 1991–2002	0.45
Built 2002 –05	0.35

ROOFS

Uninsulated

100 mm insulation*	0.45
150 mm insulation*	0.35
200 mm insulation*	0.25
100 + 150 mm insulation	0.18

GROUND FLOORS

Uninsulated	0.70
Insulated	0.45

WINDOWS

Double glazing

1990–2002	2.8
Post-2002	2.0
Pre-1990	3.3
Single glazing	5.6

rough guide is given left to U-values of different constructions, which can be used in the absence of detailed information about your home.

Lighting

Lighting circuits don't have to be in poor condition to need to be rewired; they might just be in need of a modern design makeover.

Some ceiling roses can become very busy, with several other light points connected to them. This tends to be the case with landing or hallway lights that loop out to room lights on the same floor. Because light cabling is universal in colour, red for live and black for neutral, the switch live wire becomes unexpectedly sleeved in black but is actually a live when in operation, and to overcome this a piece of red duct tape should be wrapped around it at the connections to identify its true nature. This may not have been done, so be aware of the problem and rectify it.

When it comes to locating the switches and fittings for lights, finding the right position on the wall is essential. Wall lights such as uplighters often have the lampholder and wiring exposed from above, so it is important to fix them out of reach of young hands. There are some places where they shouldn't be used, such as staircase walls where children heading down the stairs can reach in from higher steps, or even children's bedrooms, where you might choose to install sealed wall lights, such as those used in bathrooms.

When you enter a dark room you

are going to need to find that switch instinctively by touch rather than sight, and if you place it somewhere unusual, this will always result in groping around. It is best to wait for the electrical first fix (running out the cables) to start before you chalk on the wall itself the final switch position. If you close your eyes and reach out to the wall as you enter the room, you'll know where it should go. If you don't have the door fitted at the time, make sure you don't locate the switch behind the open door or too far ahead of it. It makes sense to locate switches within the accessible zone referred to in the Building Regulations: 1200 mm above floor level to the top of the plate is becoming the standard, which is better for children as well.

Wall lamps are not easily repositioned if you change your mind, since the cabling will be buried in a conduit within the wall finishings and thus inaccessible by the time the second fixing (connecting the light fittings) is done. If your wall lamps include picture lights, the positioning these must be even more critical.

Lighting tends to be forgotten about until it is too late to reap the full benefits of choice and design, but as with any home-renovation project, it needs to be pushed to the front of your mind, well ahead of the decorating. Don't let your consideration stop at where the best place to stick the switch is, and with the fitting itself waiting for the shopping spree at the very end. This is a bit of a wasted opportunity, since what matters most about lighting is getting it in the right place and achieving the right effect. Light can be stark and even, bright with contrasting shadow, soft and relaxing, and a variety of hues, if not colours.

Deciding on what you want for a particular room will mean thinking about how you plan to use that room. With kitchens, adjustable spotlights are ideal and track lights will be perfect. Bathrooms benefit from softer light to relax in, and lounges may need a variety of lighting options for reading, TV viewing and so on. In new homes there is often an astounding lack of imagination when it comes to lighting, with developers hanging a pendant fitting somewhere near the centre of each ceiling and leaving it at that. That is background lighting. It's a canvas on which you are meant to create something better, something creative and atmospheric.

Background lighting is the same as garden turfing to a developer – it's the minimum they can do to sell a new home, but to live in it you will want to improve on that. Renovation work can give you the opportunity to install cables and fittings where you've always wanted them to go, to create something unique and illuminate your home to its true potential.

Successful lighting relies on three key elements:

- The right position

- The right light source

- The right light fitting

Position

The right position for a light fitting might just be the hardest of the three elements. Ceiling lights can be used for either general lighting of a floor by being centrally placed, or as spotlights picking out reading areas or work surfaces. Tungsten-filament wall lights are great for a warm glow in a room when placed against a coloured surface, and shades like yellow and orange radiate warmth.

The right position for lights is one where a sharp glare from the lamp itself doesn't hit us in the eyes. If the lamps themselves can't be seen, just the light from them, that is good positioning. If you've ever had a glass table lamp on top of the TV you'll know what I mean – the glare of the bulb fills your retina, even when you aren't looking at it. In the early 1980s, fluorescent strip lights with their bright, stark effect were often fitted in kitchens where strong lighting is needed. They cast a shadowless even light over everything when fitted to a ceiling, and if they still have a place in the kitchen, it's hidden behind light pelmets to illuminate the worktops or ceilings above the wall cupboards.

Light source

Lamps are a lot more varied than they used to be. Not so long ago the choice was either filament bulb or fluorescent strip; now you have compact tubular fluorescent, metal halide, halogen, low and mains voltage, tungsten strips and so on. All have their merits and their purpose, so use the variety and select the right lamp for the right location.

As a general rule, the higher the wattage the brighter and whiter the light from a lamp, but the crisp sharp light of low-voltage and even mains-voltage halogen lights makes them good value for money. The very closest match to natural light however comes from metal halide lamps. If you need to spotlight something but want to avoid too much glare on it, reflector spotlamps with silvered heads or the dichroic reflector versions are what you need – standard PAR38 lamps in spots are effective, but can be a little too bright in some situations.

The colour of light

Lamps are a long way from being white all the time, but then white is not always the colour you want. Apart from the many coloured lamps available, which tend not to be made from coloured glass but from a coloured film coating the glass, the type of lamp itself has a unique hue to it, determined by its colour temperature. The lower the colour temperature, the warmer the light. Take candlelight, for example: at less than 2,000°K it is edging out of the red and into the orange end of the spectrum. Sunlight on a summer's day is in the middle of the scale, at around 5,500°K, but rising up into a blue sky away from sunlight sees the colour temperature rise to 9,000°K.

CHARACTERISTICS OF FOUR LAMP TYPES

Tungsten filament
The traditional standard bulb. Cheap to replace. Dimmable, but not efficient to run. Yellowish light of 2,700°K unless in corrective blue glass as daylight-simulation type. Comes in a variety of architectural shapes and fittings.

Tungsten halogen
The light of the millennium. Very popular since the 1990s. White and crisp light, typical in low-voltage or mains-voltage recessed spotlights. Colour temperature of around 3,000°K. Small and long-lasting, produces focused light that works well in uplighters and downlighters. The low-voltage type has better energy efficiency, but the transformers required can be a problem.

Metal halide
New to home interiors, these lamps offer high efficiency making them cheap to run. In the form of high intensity discharge (HID) they have been used in street lighting as sodium (orange glow) lamps – the most efficient light source known to man. Now also in garden spotlights. For interiors, white light halides have five times the efficiency of standard tungsten bulbs. In this form they provide the most natural light available at between 4,200 and 4,600°K. Also used in some car headlamps.

Fluorescent
● TUBULAR

The light is cold and bluish from standard fluorescents, but the new ones (T8) are far more energy-efficient than the previous T12s. Diffusers help kill the glare but look cheap and collect flies.

● COMPACT

Compact fluorescent lamps are ideal for cupboards, landings and spaces where nothing creative is needed. A warmer but duller light is created from the compact tubular types, which are highly energy-efficient and last much longer than tungsten-filament lamps. They can't be used with dimmers or PIR detectors, however.

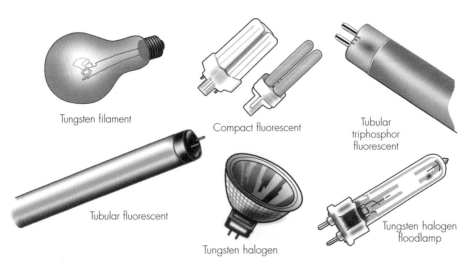

Tungsten filament

Compact fluorescent

Tubular triphosphor fluorescent

Tubular fluorescent

Tungsten halogen

Tungsten halogen floodlamp

LEDs (light-emitting diodes)

Those tungsten filament bulbs Mr Edison invented in 1878 have done well to last this long, but they are said to be 91 per cent inefficient, and because of that, they really can't stay with us for much longer. LEDs may replace them. Once the light levels from these tiny lamps are raised, they should be more available for domestic lighting. Although red pocket-calculator LED displays have been around since the 1960s, white LEDs proved elusive until 1993. Technologists are working on bringing up the lux or light from them to a useable state, and once there, they should prove to be more energy-efficient than anything we've known previously, and may even last a human lifetime. The tiny lights can be used in clusters for now and have the advantage of instant illumination, albeit rather dim.

Light fittings

Without choosing the right fitting, your choice of light source and position will have been wasted. The fitting determines how the light is directed around it and reflects the architecture of your home and its interior design. Choosing the right shade will also change the light level. One fitting you can easily change is the living room light switch – swapping it for a dimmable switch will give you the chance of altering the ambient (or background) light level. Some floor stand lamps come fitted with dimmable switches, even when they are halogen uplighters with 300W lamps, and these give you total control over ambient light.

The design of lighting

Now that we have the three ingredients for lighting, how do we use them to best effect? You can split lighting effects into five distinct techniques:

Ambient (background)

The general light reflected across a room to provide a constant level light that is functional but featureless and free from shadows is the ambient light. Outside, the ambient light would be filtered through clouds on a sunless day to be cast uniform and even on the ground. Inside, a standard ceiling pendant lamp gives us ambient light when dressed with a lampshade. Ambient light should always be dimmable to reduce its intensity and the light source should always be hidden from sight.

Accent

Because ambient light flattens everything, accent light is needed to bring some shape and texture back. You can pick out architectural features like an alcove or a fireplace, or objects like a picture or a treasured ornament. The only exception would be furniture: lighting a chair is going to draw unwanted attention on a recumbent family member, and on a table or work surface it becomes something else. Accent lighting is achievable in any room, but reception rooms are ideal for it. Spotlights, table lamps and picture lights can all be used for accent lighting, depending on how you want the feature to be displayed – so do not feel that you are limited to recessed halogen spots!

Task

Task lighting is that something else you get from lighting a chair. It sounds like it should only be employed in the kitchen or study, but when you think about it we have tasks of some kind or another to do in all rooms, and being able to see well to do those tasks is important. Task lighting needs to be bright and targeted so that the light is restricted to a particular area and doesn't spill out elsewhere. Reflective shading is used to achieve this, but it also helps if the light is directional. An example of this would be study desk lamps: being low and shaded, they cast the light down on to your desktop without spilling it around the room or up into your eyes.

Decorative

Lighting purely for decoration is not to be ignored. Whether it be the sparkle of a glass chandelier or coloured halogen lamps splashed across a wall, decorative lighting is an extension of interior decoration that complements the paint and fabrics.

For decorative light to work well the level of ambient light in the room should be low, enabling it to be seen to it's best effect. We tend to think of decorative lights as temporary, like fairy lights at Christmas, but there is no reason why in some form they can't be included permanently into your lighting scheme. Fibre-optic lights

are now available for drawing out your own starlit night onto room surfaces and large globe décor and candle bulbs have been with us for sometime.

Flame light

Flame light is the most natural form of 'artificial' lighting. The dancing flames of a fire or the flicker and glow of a candle bring a special quality that is impossible to replicate with lamps. With firelight it's the campfire security thing that reassures us we are safe from the creatures of the night, and with candlelight it's the romantic thing that reassures us that we are not safe from the creatures of the night.

The movement of light in homes needs to be kept slow, and unless artificial light gradually fades and grows it isn't pleasant. Some gas flame fires give off no heat at all but produce the necessary light effects to still make them popular.

We have grown a little unfamiliar with the risks of using fire for light, however, and candles, oil burners and real fires need care and attention if they aren't to become accidents. Naked flames need to be positioned carefully and treated with some respect more than anything else, so give some thought to what sits above a candle or an oil burner before you light it – a wooden shelf? A curtain? They may seem out of reach, but the heat alone from the flame could blacken them or worse ignite them, even without its touch.

To my absolute amazement, 'cool fires' are now described in interior design magazines and there are manufacturers producing 'fireplaces' that offer neither firelight or heat. Instead of coals or wood the hearth basket may be filled with blue glass chips or polished white stones, and lit by accent lighting the fires allegedly give off the opposite of heat – a hearth to sit by on a hot summer day; a sort of anti- fireplace. As a focal point I see that, but cool fire – please; if you want cheap air-conditioning, leave the fridge door open.

The amount of light

Before deciding on what light source you need, you might want to experiment with an extension cable and various lamps to see just how much light or lux each can generate. Not only will this give you some idea of the type of lamp you'll need, but also the wattage or power required; the only problem is it that it will be difficult to visualise the final effect until the decorating is complete. White walls bounce back about 70 per cent of the light, dark ones only 30 per cent. Grey slate floors absorb all but 10 ten per cent of the light shone on them. As a rough guide, dining rooms need about 50 lux (just enough to stop you knocking over the wine but still enough to be able to see what you're eating), kitchens should have about 300 lux and stairways should also be close to this level for safety.

The spread of light is also an issue, and for this you need to be aware of the angle of the beam generated by a particular lamp. The packaging should reveal this. Those low-halogen spots we peppered our ceilings with in the late 1990s may only have 35W of power, but they shed about 500 lux to the floor directly below. However, with a low-angle beam they don't spread that light so very far.

For the same amount of lux, but from a higher wattage source and spread over a greater area, you might choose a PAR38 flood lamp. PAR38 reflector lamps are made from cast glass, making them fairly weighty, and with perhaps a 30° beam angle, these lights, fixed in recessed ceiling mountings, can cover a large area of floor 3 m. Be careful not to confuse then with spot PAR38s, which might appear identical but have a much narrower beam. The latter make better task lights aimed at kitchen worktops or narrow floors like landings to stairs, with a flood type being positioned over the stairs itself.

Lamps and heat

Heat is an unfortunate by-product of many modern lamps. Halogen and dichroic reflector lamps produce a lot of it and need to be placed at a suitable distance from their subject. This is particularly important when using them in display cabinets. The fact that they may be small belies how hot they get, and having recently burned the back of my hand in a shop display cabinet lamp, I can testify to that. No, I wasn't doing research.

The trend to recess lights into ceilings brings one other unfortunate risk of fire spread. Our ceilings offer some fire resistance to upper floors, and cutting out an array of holes in them doesn't do much to maintain that fire resistance. Dichroics throw the heat backward through the glass and shouldn't be fitted in ceilings without fire-protective covers. These small hoods prevent the heat from being transferred to the structure and charring it; they also act to 'repair' the hole in the fire-resisting ceiling.

In the United States uplighters with halogen lamps in them gave rise to so many house fires that it soon became required for manufacturers to fit protectors over them. As plug-in floor stand lights they might house 300W halogens that get a little hot. If they stand 2 m off the floor, however, leaving 500 mm–1 m to the ceiling, not much harm can come to them. Using these beneath galleries or higher coved ceilings would be inappropriate usage.

Outdoor lighting

As we've been taking a greater interest in renovating our gardens, we not only want to spend more time in them, we want to light them and enjoy them from inside as well as out. Garden lighting needs to be just as carefully planned as the lighting in our rooms, so that the best features of the garden are revealed. Accent lighting using garden spotlamps is an effective way to achieve this, and helps to keep the lamps low and close to the subject. This should help to avoid light spilling off into other parts of the garden or your neighbours' garden and generally making a nuisance of itself. Uplighting can sometimes need a baffle or a shield of some kind to prevent it from oversailing the object you are aiming

to light. You can reduce the amount of spread laterally by choosing spots over floods or by using a tube (like a short piece of drainpipe) over a ground lamp as a baffle.

Light pollution has left us living beneath an iridescent glow that covers the night sky, blanking out the stars. Starlight has a long way to travel to reach us, and it seems sad that after a journey of hundreds, if not thousands, of years, we blank it out in the last few seconds.

Resist the urge to screw 500W halogen floodlights on to the walls of your home with PIR detectors that scan half the garden and the pavement going by. They may be enticingly cheap, but the aggravation they cause is expensive, and besides that, the wall of light they create will do nothing to improve your home and has even been said to reduce security by providing too much glare. Think about it: our pupils enlarge in the dark to see better and dilate when they meet bright light, which means we see less in the dark shadows outside it.

150W halogen lamps, such as those in the mini-flood range, are far more effective. You can use them closer to the area you want to light and control the detection zone more tightly. I have one placed that faces directly down beneath the porch roof to my summerhouse. Both the lamp and the PIR are hidden from sight and are only activated by movement close to the door face, so the light only comes on when I enter or leave the summerhouse, when the pool of light bathes the porch area to no more than a square metre or two. If you have an open porch or a wide overhang to your roof, using a PAR38 or mini-flood vertically down like this is very effective. To reduce glare, the angle of the beam should be below 70° anyway, but the nearer to vertical the better.

Trees shouldn't be hit with bright white lights at night, if nothing else because this will disturb roosting wildlife. To grab an occasional effect from the oak wood bordering my garden, I've aimed one coloured PAR-38-reflector floodlight up from below the overhanging trees. The light is triggered only by low-level PIR that is activated by the cats and other creatures prowling. It's enough to be very effective, and although only sporadic, all the more enjoyable for it.

White light is by far the most creative option, so I would save the urge to challenge the Blackpool Illuminations for Christmas and not use too much colour in flood or spot lamps. Give some thought as well to the light spilling out from your windows and doors. It will reach a certain distance in to the garden but after that if you want to entertain out of its reach you will need to find a way of bringing the light to you. If you have the room for them, table lamps are ideal when you're eating, and better still are small globe lights that can be clipped to the underside of a parasol. Having a garden socket outlet in a favourite spot will give you the ability to bring light wherever you want and give you the freedom to eat out after dark.

If you've spent any time looking for your car in a multi-storey car park at night, you'll know that fluorescent strip lights are great for security, as they give off an even bright light, but terrible for colour. The cold blueness of their colour temperature also makes them unsympathetic to plants and too functional. For the garden, metal halide, tungsten and halogen are the only choices, and of the three, metal halide is by far the most energy-efficient for 'theatrical' lighting.

You can use daylight sensors to bring on the lights at night, but they will do this all night, so it is better to use a timer to automatically switch on and off the lighting at times when it's most appreciated.

What to light at night

When deciding what elements of your garden to light, look for unique and interesting features – a stone, a palm or a clump of bamboo. Look for shape and texture over colour, which beyond green will appear less than colourful outside daylight. What you really need is a striking subject with some structure to it. Plants described as 'architectural' in planting schemes are perfect, and include:

Palms
Ferns
Grasses
Phormiums
Cordylines
Gunnera manicata
Eucalyptus
Cycas
Fatsia

CHAPTER FIVE

Replumbing

Bathroom renovation

Not so very long ago, renovating a bathroom would have meant replacing a cracked toilet seat or adding a medicine cabinet with fancy mirror doors. If you really wanted to push the boat out, you'd have one with a built-in light. Not any more – bathrooms are design ventures now. The smallest room in the house might be the last room in the house to receive the interior design treatment, but it has plenty of opportunity in it. This is not just a room to clean and exercise your bodily functions in, it is also a room to relax and recharge, to 'freshen and invigorate the mind and body' – you have to admit it, the 21st-century bathroom is a new place.

For starters, the shower is replacing the bath in popularity, but you really need both – you can't read a book in the shower, not even this one. I accept that not everybody agrees with the need for both, and with the advent of larger and more stylish shower enclosures, some of us have been ripping out the bath altogether and replacing it with a shower. Standard baths are usually 1.7 m long, and a replacement shower can use all this with stylish patterned glass screening and ceramic tiles, for a head-height spray, total body massage and sauna-mode facility.

Renovating any bathroom, even without fitting a state-of-the-art shower, often involves new appliances in new positions, and it is amazing how much plumbing has to be done to replace a WC, even when it's in the same position. It would be nice to think that you could just whip the old one out and slot the new one in, with all the pipes lining up for a quick and easy jointing – nice, but maybe in some other world. WCs are all different, and their size has changed a lot in recent years. Smaller and more stylish, they can fit into corners or tight spaces now, but this all means that the plumbing serving them will have to be changed to fit the one you've bought.

If you can rejig the layout of the bathroom to make it much more agreeable, don't be persuaded not to. Plumbing will be altered anyway, so you might as well go the whole hog and alter it for the better. Simply switching the position of an appliance from one wall to another can improve the access to the room immeasurably. There are limits to how far waste pipes can run unvented, but they can be extended with air-admittance valves, and usually it is the fall of a pipe or the structure of the floor that limits where appliances can go. Showers are notoriously difficult because of the low position of the traps. It often means that the trays have to be raised (on extra joists or concrete blocks) above floor level to get the pipework in. Stone-cast trays are best bedded in sand and cement mortar, so using blocks to raise them is ideal.

Alterations to the water supply

Not the drinking water but the cold and hot water supply to your appliances will need extending or altering to some extent, and this presents you with a choice of materials.

Copper tubing

Armed with the right tools and plenty of patience, copper tube plumbing is an achievable and traditional way to lay water pipes. The joints are soldered together with a round wire solder, but first the tubes have to be cut clean and square with a pipe cutter and then cleaned off with wire wool. A chemical cleaner (non-corrosive and paste-like) known as flux is then used to clean the ends to be jointed. The pipes are then joined and heated up with a blowtorch until the flux begins to bubble before the solder is wound around the mouth of the joint. This then gets heated up to the right temperature and is allowed to cool into a solid sleeve, and bingo, the joint is formed. You get to do this, not just to join straight pipe, but for every bend, T and elbow. Now you see why plastic plumbing is popular.

Plastic tubing

In the same way that you don't see many careless electricians, you don't see many happy plumbers. Actually, I did see a happy plumber the other day, but then he had only recently qualified and hadn't had the chance to accrue the years of misery that can only come with joining water pipes together for a living. You're thinking they should be happy given the charge-out rate for their work, so maybe they don't like to show it. On any given building site you can usually hear the plumber bitching over a leaking joint as he works. I sympathise with them; anything to do with pressure and water is likely to be trouble, which is why I applaud any new products in the plumbing world that make life easier, and lately there have been quite a few.

Plumbing in a water supply and waste-water drainage is becoming more and more suited for DIY, largely due to the advent of plastic push-fit pipe systems to complement the original copper tubing – 'complement' because it can be joined to it – there's no need to replumb the entire house.

The copper-tube system has never been in the reach of the amateur plumber. It doesn't require expensive tools – a blowtorch and a pipe bender will get you by – but it does take some practice and skill to weld joints properly. When you're working on your own home, practice isn't an option, especially when your water supply and heating system is at stake. The one big drawback with plumbing work is that you only get to find out whether it works after you've turned the water back on, and that's when it all goes wrong.

Compression jointing is possible in lieu of soldering but it requires a degree of access to get at all the fittings and makes the joints rather bulky. If you overtighten the nuts, the olives will crack and the joint will leak. Compression joints have to be just as carefully formed to be watertight.

Altering the copper tube system or extending it in quick-fit plastic does have some advantages for both the amateur and professional plumber. First, the pipe can either be bought in manageable lengths of around 2 m or in longer coiled lengths of 25 m, from which it can be cut and joined. To my simple mind and even simpler plumbing skills the fewer the joints the better, and long lengths of pipe that can be fed through between floor joists and wall cavities really don't want to be jointed at all.

It tends to be a water authority bylaw that in walls pipes aren't jointed – this relates to their inaccessibility when leaks occur. In solid ground floors it means laying them inside ducts but with floor joists, the floorboards can be lifted and qualify as accessible, although you might disagree. The great thing about plastic is that it bends a bit, and although there are elbows and Ts where it doesn't, given enough clips and space it bends nicely.

Pipe inserts are used to join cut pipes, which need to be de-burred carefully (for which a special de-burring tool is available), and the fittings are designed to be locked together with a simple push or twist action. Special tools are needed to separate them, so make sure you lay out your system carefully before you join it up.

Plastic can be joined to existing copper with adapters, and likewise copper can be joined to plastic for things that are on show, like radiator tail-pipes. The disadvantage of plastic is as it always has been – that it looks like plastic. Not only that, but the pipes used for the hot and cold water supply are manufactured and graded differently to those used for heating systems, so be aware of the grading.

As if this isn't enough, one other choice exists – push-fit copper tubing. This traditional material used with a new and advanced jointing method is a little more expensive, but it could just be worth it.

Waste pipes

Waste-pipe plumbing has three systems to offer: solvent-weld, compression and push-fit.

Solvent-weld

Solvent-welding the joints of waste plumbing may have put off some DIY plumbers, but it shouldn't have. The trick with solvent welding is to make sure everything is fitted together as it should be and as you want it with the appliances connected up before you go around and take each joint apart for the gluing. Do not be tempted to glue it up as you go, because solvent-weld doesn't come apart after it has set, at least not without a saw. The pipes with this system are thicker and stronger, and it does look a lot more professional when complete, but it isn't the only choice.

Compression joints

These are a more DIY-friendly option that allow you to assemble and dismantle the system until you get it right. They are easily removed and refitted. No glues, or tools come to that, are required. The joints are tightened, and so long as the chamfered rubber seals are not

Appliance	Waste pipe size of waste	Max length	Trap size	Standard fall
WC	100 mm	6 m	50 mm	20 mm
Bath	40 mm	3 m	50 mm	20–40 mm
Shower	40 mm	3 m	50 mm	20–40 mm
Basin	32 mm	1.7 m	75 mm	20 mm
Combined	50 mm	4 m	——	20–40 mm

pinched or misshaped, they shouldn't leak. The fittings, such as elbows and T-pieces, are a bit bulkier than the other types, and you do need fairly good access to get at them, which basically means you can't fit them tight up against a wall. For these reasons I've always thought that a combination of compression fittings and push-fit ones is a better option.

Push-fit

Push-fit in waste-water plumbing isn't the same as the push-fit in water pipes where pressure is at work. In this case the joints don't snap-lock in place – quite the opposite, as they just slide together; and the thickness in the wall of the pipe is reduced compared to the solvent and compression systems. The system isn't compatible with solvent-weld pipes because of this reduced diameter. Compression fittings can accommodate both solvent-weld and push-fit ones if you have to extend an existing system, and that can make them ideal for renovation projects. Push-fit pipes can be kinked because of this and are

unintentionally bendable, which I find troubling. This lack of strength must mean they need plenty of support if hot waste water is to flow through them without the pipe sagging. What is really needed is a push-and-twist lock system for waste-water plumbing that combines the strength and quality of solvent-weld with speed of fitting.

The fall on waste pipes of 32–50 mm diameter should be somewhere between 18 mm and 90 mm per 1 m run. Outside these limits, problems may occur.

With 100 mm pipes for WC pans, the fall should be at the lower gradient of 18 mm per 1 m for a single WC, but if you have long runs of waste and more than one pan connected you could reduce this to 9 mm per 1 m.

One of the greatest problems with renovating existing plumbing systems is having to work with the general layout. Often this means cast-iron external pipework that includes hoppers collecting rainwater plus basin and bath wastes halfway up the wall. We stopped allowing waste water into open hoppers some years ago;

since they have no trap, they allow foul air to vent out. If you can replace them with a sealed fitting when renewing a waste running to them, do so. My only concern before you do this would be to check that the system is still vented properly.

Large Victorian terraced homes often have a veritable network of waste pipes encircling the walls. As the table on page 99 shows, waste runs have limits if they are to remain ventilated and the water is to be maintained in the traps. If they exceed these limits, added vents are needed to the branches. Many extended WC branch pipes only work because they have hopper-headed pipes running off them, ventilating the branch. (Hoppers are box-like terminations at the top of pipes that help collect open water; they were very popular for bringing basin and bath wastes to in the past, but this is no longer acceptable.)

Joining up plastic soil and vent pipes to an existing cast iron system was never easy, but we now have universal-fit connectors, large rubber collars fixed with stainless steel jubilee clips. Mostly used below ground, they don't look pretty above it, but drainage never does.

Most soil and vent systems come in grey that fades to pale grey in about 20 years, which is a shame because black is often needed to connect into existing systems – particularly cast-iron. If you want black, specify it and make sure your plumber allows enough time to order it. It is available, but maybe not from his regular supplier. So many

plumbers give you the option of painting the pipework whatever colour you want after they've gone, rather than supply it to begin with. Black, white and grey are the standard options, as brown is reserved for rainwater and reddish brown is for below-ground drains only. For conservation-minded renovation, aluminium systems are often black and look far superior to PVC-U on period homes.

As mentioned earlier, with wastewater pipework to stop the water seals in traps from being broken (pulled out) by the air pressures that can exist in the system, maximum lengths apply. You can exceed these lengths by ventilating the branch waste runs, either by introducing a vent pipe to them or, more commonly, by fitting an air-admittance valve (AAV) to the pipe. These devices draw air into the system when it's needed to aid the flow of water and protect the traps. You can buy them as 100 mm fittings to go on top of stub stacks (shortened SVPs), or as smaller diameters to go on bath and basin waste pipes. They are very useful on 40 mm shower wastes, where en-suite showers are being installed some distance from the existing drainage system and the pipe run would exceed 3 m.

If you have a WC that needs to be connected further than 6 m away from the soil vent stack pipe, a stub stack terminated with an AAV is what you need to install.

These products have a rubber seal inside them which could freeze up if fitted outside, so you are restricted to internal stacks. Bear this in mind, because some plumbers are prone to using them to get out of trouble. For example, when a normal vent would be beneath a window or within 3 m of the side of one, rather than taking the pipe up high to get well above it, the AAV seems like a attractive solution. When external-use types that don't freeze are made they will be popular; until then they can go in the loft space or indoors, but that's all.

Stub stacks serve another purpose, giving you a fighting chance of getting all your other waste pipes into the one pipe. Try to avoid connecting waste pipes into stacks directly opposite each other; a staggered connection or a proprietary boss connector should be used to make sure you don't get foul water from one running full into the other.

Floor-level manifolds are good but when you're working in an existing home with given levels, they can't always fit in. WC pan connectors are available with smaller waste pipe sockets on the bend to take a basin or shower. Stub stacks give you about 1 m high of soil stack to connect to. If you can run pipes through floors do so, but that means between joists; cutting out notches or holes for even a 32 mm pipe is not acceptable and will weaken the floor disastrously. Surface pipework isn't pretty, but it can be painted in to match walls or woodwork, and unless you are going to build in the WC cistern, some exposed pipework is inevitable. It's easy to become obsessed with the

idea of encasing all the pipes in a bathroom, but I'm not sure if many people would notice. So long as it looks tidy and the majority of pipes are hidden from view, most of us who aren't plumbers would be happy.

Boxing-in pipework has been something of an obsession, but frankly much boxing looks as bad as exposed pipes would. The only true solution is to use plenty of forethought when locating appliances, and if need be bring in a false wall as a service duct. Using 50 x 50 mm studwork and plasterboard, creating a false wall at least 120 mm in front of the original wall will give you the chance to conceal all the pipes. As far as I know, only two things will stop you doing this:

● You'll lose at least 180 mm off the room dimensions.

● You'll need all your appliances plumbed to the same wall in order to hide everything.

One other thing: you need access panels for maintenance – access to the important water supply for isolating valves to be turned on and off, and to waste drainage at changes or direction for cleaning. Stub stacks and AAVs can be boxed in, but bear in mind that they need to draw in air, so leave some gaps or include a vent grill somewhere. You might use some vented PVC-U soffit board to clad it with if tiling isn't for you.

Once all the pipes are connected up and your appliances are fitted, the system should be air-tested to check for any leaks. Plumbers have the equipment needed for this, and you need to ensure that they test their own work and notify the Building Control Officer to witness the test. This is one of those Building Regulation statutory inspections that are vital to you receiving your Completion Certificate later.

If you've carried out the plumbing work yourself, you can buy or hire the equipment. You will need at least two 100 mm adjustable bungs to seal off the stack at the top and bottom in the first manhole, and possibly a manometer to measure the air pressure in the system. Bags that can be inflated in pipes are an alternative to bungs. With all the traps full of water and nothing left open or unconnected (at washing machine or dishwasher waste points), it should be possible to push up the gauge gently with air to at least 38 mm and hold it there for three minutes or more.

It is possible to carry out an effective air test on plumbing by filling the WC or sink bowl with water. If the pipes are airtight, it won't drain away. Gazing into the pan at the water level for a few minutes to check that it doesn't drop is one of the few pleasures in the world of plumbing, and it is easy to drift into a reflective trance. Using a matchstick or marking the side of the pan with a pencil will help you focus on the job at hand.

Testing in this way has one other benefit. It also checks the pan itself for any flaws and is the only way of discovering whether the pan has a hairline crack in the china – when

pans do, it is almost impossible to see.

You might choose to fill the pan by flushing the cistern, but it is entirely possible to flood your home by doing this, particularly if you use an upstairs WC and the pressure forces water out downstairs, or if you have an open washing machine waste in the kitchen. Proceed carefully, filling the pan slowly if you can – you are dealing with pressure and water here, two of the worst things known to man.

Renewing bathroom appliances

When you move in to anything but a brand-new home, there is often no more pressing a task than to replace the bathroom appliances. The idea of using somebody else's toilet and bath is a difficult one for a lot of people, and if they happen to be a bit 'worn', shall we say, or the colour of avocado, then they've got to go.

Bathroom style

Most manufacturers offer complete suites in a particular style, not just all the appliances but all the accessories, right down to the loo roll holder and the soap dish.

The range of styles is growing, and as always, fashion is playing a part. At the millennium the Victorian style, with its opulent brassware taps and white high-level cisterns, was all the rage, along with showers of rigid riser pips and single-lever capstans that drop a deluge of water from a large rose. Simple and unadjustable, they are always stylish and suit any home, especially Victorian houses.

Contemporary glass basin.

In 2004 the trend is growing towards the contemporary style of glass bowl basins and chrome. Contemporary has curves and sweeping lines, but is simple and uncluttered, with no fancy trims. Rope trim and shell styles were around before the Victorians, but they are still here and available to those who want a classic design. As with kitchens, colours come and go, but white seems timeless and clean, and you can add colour to any bathroom with the walls and furnishings.

In Britain, the one thing holding us back is the size of our bathrooms, which have always been small and are getting smaller. There may be have more of them, with en-suites and cloakrooms, but unless you have converted a spare bedroom, they tend to be less than spacious. It gives us an excuse not to have a bidet, if nothing else.

WC style

Close-coupled loos are by far the most popular, partly because they use up less space. Without the flush pipe to bring the pan forward, they are that extra bit compact and tidy. Flush pipes were never pretty anyway. The one drawback of some close-coupled pans is that not all toilet seats and lids will stay up; it's all in the hinges because they stand almost vertical to the cistern. Corner WCs are available for a space-saving en-suite, but at tremendous expense.

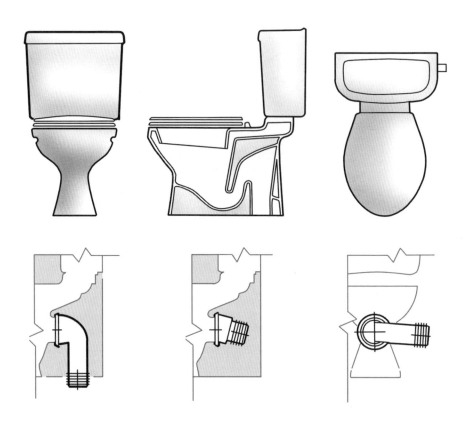

Conventional WC pan and varied pan connectors.

Bath style

A cheaper option than buying a new or fully restored cast-iron bath is to buy one to restore yourself. Architectural salvage yards often sell original cast-iron tubs in rusted and ruined condition, but with a lot of elbow action they can be brought back into use. Refurbishment kits are available, but they don't contain any miracles of salvation – you still need to apply hard work, armed with wet and dry abrasive paper, rust inhibitor and epoxy filler. The filler is for the chips and scratches, but most of the restoration process appears to involve rubber gloves, cleaning agents and continuous sanding.

Cast-iron bathtubs are heavy, and I've met one home-owner who bought one (apparently Harold Macmillan's) and had to use a crane to install it

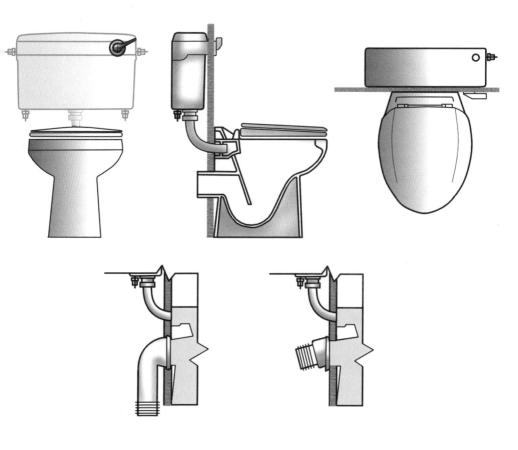

Concealed cistern WC.

through a first-floor window. Measure your stairs and door widths before you buy. The floor structure may need to be strengthened with additional joists and floor-grade plywood beforehand, if the bathtub isn't to be instantly relocated on the ground floor.

If you're not going for the cast-iron centrepiece roll-top bath for your Victorian bathroom, a standard bath might seem a poor relation to choose.

You do, however, have the option of a contemporary hydro-bath. For a while it looked like hydrotherapy might just be for senior citizens, but now it has caught on and baths with spa jets to massage you are great for relaxing in. Some are designed with focused pressure jets all round – back, neck and sides, even at the foot end, so that instead of exercising your toes by sticking them in the taps you can have

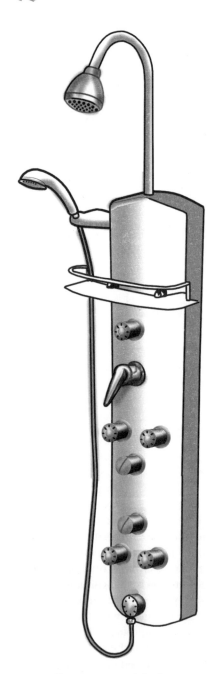

Shower tower with body jets.

then pummelled reflexology-style. Many are fitted with an underwater light so can you see where the bubbles are going – how cool is that?

Shower style

The shower experience can be more than just streaming hot or cold water from above; it can be steam and body jets as well. Shower tower cabins are complete plastic cubicles that have directional body jets built into the walls. Moulded in plastic throughout, they have the benefit of being leak-free, which is precious with a first-floor shower, and many include seats and facilities for converting the shower to a steam room. With the latter you get a roof to the cubicle for the complete Tupperware box experience that won't fill your bathroom with steam.

The ease of installation counts for a lot with these; you simply fix them to the wall and connect up the hot and cold water. They work best with unvented water systems, but don't forget just how much water they deliver – the average shower uses 35 l of water compared to 90 l in one of these. A little more space is needed than with a standard shower, and a good deal more money, but I have no doubt they will become cheaper as more and more of us buy them.

Sauna style

If you have the space, the last luxury item for the renovated bathroom is a sauna. Now available to home-owners in a compact size for one or two people, a Finnish timber sauna

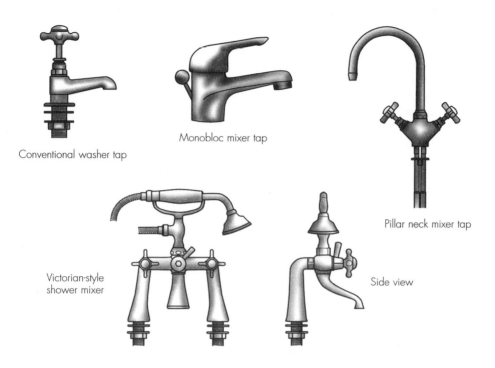

Conventional washer tap

Monobloc mixer tap

Pillar neck mixer tap

Victorian-style
shower mixer

Side view

Choose a tap style that suits the appliance and the room.

converts your bathroom into a health club. Invariably these cubicle models use electric sauna stoves rated between 3 and 6 kW (less than a serious electric shower). I would have thought that, given the shed-like design, it would be possible to build your own sauna with some tongue-and-groove timber boarding, a glass door and an electric sauna stove; but I have yet to meet anyone who has.

Taps

Taps have been pieces of art for a while – half the taps sold in the UK are imported, and price-wise you can pay what you like. It has to be said,

however, that the same products in France, for example, are sold at a fraction of the price. The technology in taps hasn't changed since washers were replaced by ceramic discs; all that's happened since about 1990 is that architecture has allowed them to become designer products. They have become difficult to service and maintain now, and most, regardless of price, are ultimately disposable. Make sure you fit service valves in line to the water pipes, which will make it easier to replace them when you've grown tired of their style.

The hot water produced by modern cylinders and boilers is jolly hot and can easily scald us. Children and senior citizens are even more at risk from scalding water, which, contrary to popular belief, doesn't have to be boiling to cause serious harm.

The temperature of your cold water supply should never rise to more than 25°C, and it shouldn't be more than 3°C warmer at the taps than it is at the tank. Warm water for drinking can be a problem to say the least. Legionellis (Legionnaires Disease) breeds in water of a certain temperature (somewhere between 25° and 45°C), and for this reason alone hot water should be stored in cylinders at around 60°C.

All very well, but that's too hot to be running from the taps without the risk of scalding – at 60°C it takes only seven seconds to burn our skin, and at 70°C it takes only a second.

Thermostatic taps overcome this by regulating the temperature to a predetermined setting. Most are factory-set to 43°C and prevent water in excess of this temperature from being delivered. In shower units, mixers with thermostats are essential, but because of the risk of bacteria multiplying at this temperature, water that has passed through the thermostat can't run through pipes longer than 2 m, which governs the length of shower head pipes, just in case you were thinking of creating your own self-plumbed advanced deluge shower head with a 3 m length of water main. I totally understand if you were – I am amazed at how much can be charged for what is basically a piece of bent pipe with a watering

can rose at one end on the grounds that is of Victorian style.

Although most thermostatic taps are pre-set at 45°C, whether they are showers, basin or bath taps, they can normally be adjusted to suit your needs, and you may have to turn some up to balance the mix if cold-water pressure exceeds hot-water pressure.

Radiators

We are used to ignoring our radiators even more than our ceilings. Rooms that have been faithfully renovated in Victorian décor and furnishings are heated by the steel panel convector radiator on the wall. You don't have to cover these with MDF radiator covers any more, as radiators have now been given the design treatment as well. To be fair, there are limits, and until recently the range of radiators has been a bit limited, to say the least, but many more styles are available now.

For Victorian-style heating you can look in reclamation yards and hunt for the original cast-iron boiler-house radiator that weighs more than the wall you want to hang it on. If you find it, chances are it will need shotblasting to shift a hundred years of paint before it can be painted again and then plumbed in with large-diameter pipe. Or you could buy one of the new replica models in the modern stove-enamelled steel equivalent, in the same style but a little less overweight. Invariably they are both floor- and wall-mounted.

For contemporary décor, the choice expands greatly with chrome or white finishes and wave-shaped wall-hung

A ROUGH GUIDE TO RADIATOR OUTPUTS/SIZES FOR GIVEN ROOM SIZES

Room size	BTUs/hr	Kilowatts/hr	Single panel	Double panel
2.4 x 2.4 m	4,100	1.2	620 x 1100 mm	
3.6 x 3.0 m	6,400	1.9	620 x 1700 mm	
4.8 x 3.6 m	8,900	2.6		620 x 1250 mm
5.5 x 4.2 m	11,000	3.2		620 x 1600 mm
6.1 x 5.5 m	14,200	4.2		620 x 2000 mm

MULTIPLY THE RATED OUTPUTS BY THE FOLLOWING FACTORS TO CORRECT THESE:

Reduce by		Increase by	
Cavity walls	−10%	Two outside walls	+15%
Insulated cavity walls	−20%	Three outside walls	+40%
Double glazing	−5%	North-facing	+10%

types that can be floor-to-ceiling sized or low-level. Radiators in contemporary style renovations can themselves be used as pieces of art, with sculptured coils and rings in chrome plating set into the room's corners, or curved cut-outs of walls with accent lighting at the top and bottom. Instead of being invisible, these radiators are focal points. Some at the 'designer' end of the market are made to look like plants, while others are coated with an anodised finish on which artwork can be graphically reproduced. Using these, you can design in your own finish for a totally unique look.

We have had an insatiable urge for towel warmers in recent years. The market for towel radiators has expanded as well, but if you need one to heat a bathroom as well as the towels, you are going to have to find an oversized one. The act of covering a radiator with a towel will prevent a lot of heat escaping anyway, but towel radiators don't give off a huge amount of heat, usually only in the region of 500W. It obviously helps if your bathroom is well insulated in the walls and roof, but older terraced homes, for example, where your bathroom is a back addition or a converted bedroom, struggle to be heated by just a towel radiator. Without sufficient insulation and heating, these rooms tend to suffer from condensation, and trying to assuage these conditions with a towel radiator is not going to work.

If you have the room for a convector radiator as well, use both, but if you don't you may need a combination radiator that has a convection panel and a towel rail or two along the top – the perfect space-saver solution that heats the room and the towels. Some manufacturers have responded to this lack of space by producing over-the-bath models that make use of the wall aside the bathtub.

When deciding on any radiator, look at the rated output in watts and the heat loss from the room. For radiators to work as intended, they should be capable of maintaining a room temperature of 21°C when the outside air temperature is –5°C. Try to avoid a situation where too powerful a radiator is needed – bathroom nudity and hot lumps of metal are not a happy combination.

The table on page 109 can be used as a rough guide to radiator sizes, based on output for given room sizes. It assumes the room is heated to 21°C and has one external solid brick wall with an average-size window, 2.4 m ceiling height and 100 mm of loft insulation to the ceiling.

Or calculate the heat loss from your room more accurately using the elemental U-values given on page 87 and multiply them by the respective area of each element.

Making room for a shower

Apart from the fact that most of us seem to prefer showers to baths, there is much more chance of finding room for a shower in renovation work. The only place showers don't seem to fit is under the stairs or in a loft conversion, where the ceiling headroom isn't available. Even the modern home, with its 2.3-m ceilings, can still house a shower after the tray has been raised to get the plumbing in. Which is a lead to the first point of design. For the moment forget about what type of shower you want, they all need one basic thing – drainage. The shower tray must have a waste run that connects to the drainage system, and there are limits.

More importantly, there are falls. If you're connecting up the shower waste pipe with other existing waste pipes, then their height will determine the height of the shower tray. It is possible to form a step up to the shower if you have the room, but otherwise you won't want to raise the tray more than 100 mm or so above the floor level. If you only have so much headroom left between the tray and the ceiling your next question is, did I really want a Victorian-style fixed shower head that I have to stand directly beneath, or is a wall-mounted adjustable head on a slider rail that hits you in the face, rather than on the cranium, a better option? The answer is yes – if that's all that fits.

Mixer or electric?

Hold that thought while you consider the hot-water situation in your home.

Mixer showers that are fed by your hot-water supply demand a certain level of performance. A vented system may not store enough hot water in the cylinder to run a shower, or a combi might not produce a high enough flow rate to trigger its ignition. Combis also have a relatively low flow rate, and the shower will run cold if somebody runs the bath or sink tap while you're in there. Ask me how annoying that is.

If the pressure isn't there, you can't add a pump to convert it to a power shower unless you have a gravity (vented) system with a high-volume storage tank.

Some showers are described as 'combi compatible' and some aren't, but if your combi doesn't have an adjustable flow-rate switch or your shower doesn't deliver enough flow, you might need to have the heating on and the boiler running before it works. Another common failing is with the cold-water (mains) pressure, which may arrive in the mixer shower too strongly for it to be able to cope, and you may have to buy a flow-restrictor later to reduce it. Shower manufacturers do not go to any lengths to tell you the limitations of their products, but doing as much research before you buy can save a lot of time, effort and hassle later.

The very best hot-water system for showers is the unvented storage cylinder or thermal store. These large-volume cylinders can produce plenty of hot water at pressure for more than one appliance at a time. Pumps or power showers are not possible with unvented water systems like these.

In spite of the reservations, a mixer shower should still be your first choice. They last longer and don't submit to hard water and limescale quite so quickly or fatally as electric showers. With a mixer, you take out the pump and de-scale once a year, but with an electric shower you throw it away and buy another one. Consider how often you replace your electric kettle, and that's how often you'll need to replace your electric shower – they are, when all is said and done, basically the same appliance with an element to heat up the water. Some are made to be easily replaced with a choice of cable and pipe connecting points or even flexible or moveable points to try and suit your service entry positions, so these seem like a good choice. Alternatively, buy two of the same showers and put one in the shed in reserve. You can thank me later when you come to replace it.

The benefit of an electric shower is that it doesn't care what type of plumbing system you have, so long as you can get a cold-water pipe to it. If you live in a hard water area, buy a cheap one with the most powerful rated output you can get. A 10.5 kW shower with a higher flow rate will bear the effects of limescale build-up for longer, simply because the flow rate has more capacity to be reduced than, say, an 8 kW shower. The higher the kilowatt rating the more powerful the shower, but you can still expect performance to be reduced in winter, when the incoming water supply is colder than in summer.

Upgrading an existing shower with a pump

If your home already has a mixer shower fed by a gravity system but you're unhappy with its flow rate, you might be able to boost it by adding a pump. This could mean, however, that you have to replace the water tanks with larger ones, or your shower may run out of water before you've had a chance to enjoy it.

How much water does a power shower use? You can look at the litres per minute flow rate on the pack and work out your showering time given your cylinder size. A 120 l cylinder will supply a shower with a flow rate of 12 l per minute for ten minutes. Pumps push up the flow rate so much (some of these pumps run up to 3 bar of pressure, and this will dramatically increase the flow rate) that showering time can be brief.

Typically a 900 mm high x 450 mm diameter hot water tank stores about 120 l of water, and a 1050 mm high x 450 mm diameter tank stores about 144 l. It isn't really possible to consider using water tanks below 12 l for supplying showers, as they don't achieve the showering time that most of us consider to be the minimum.

Electricity supply

Electric showers need a high cable rating and a separate connection to the consumer unit. The electricity supply cannot be taken off the 30-amp ring main that serves the power outlets. The manufacturer's instructions will give you the current rating of the circuit needed for it, and you can expect that to increase with the rated output. A 10.5 kW shower typically needs a 45-amp circuit, but a 7.5 kW one may only need a 35-amp circuit with a corresponding fuse or MCB protection.

Check to make sure that your consumer unit has a spare fuseway and that it has a rating of at least 80 amps. If it doesn't, you have a larger job than you thought – the unit may have to be replaced with a new or a separate individual unit installed to serve this circuit. Neither of these tasks is impossible, but they should be carried out by a registered electrician.

The supply must be delivered via a switched connection unit, which allows it to be switched off when any maintenance work is required to the shower (or it needs replacing), although the fuse or MCB at the distribution board should also be removed prior to this.

Shower trays

Trays tend to be either cast stone or HDF, the former a mixture of limestone and resin that makes for a solid base to stand on that won't bend when you step in, while the latter is high-density plastic foam that will. The stone ones can chip and the plastic ones can crack; those that are acrylic-finished are said not to scratch, but at the end of the day I'm sure that's possible if you try hard enough.

Screens can be curved or square, plastic or glass. For some reason the plastic ones, made of clear acrylic, are labelled safety glass and not safety plastic. Glass implies quality and is less prone to scratching so don't rely on the labelling: pick it up and see how heavy it is. Doors can be pivoting, sliding or bi-folding, and they can be considered watertight in that order, although quality pays off in this area.

It's a fact that most site-built showers leak. Tiles are waterproof but tiling grout isn't, no matter what it says on the pot, and the mastic-sealed joints at the bases and corners are always a weak point. Getting your shower watertight may take time and a process of elimination, but you can do a few things to begin with that will reduce the leaks and the stress.

First, if you're forming a shower cubicle in timber studwork, do not board it with plasterboard for tiling over. Use a water-resistant external board like OSB (orientated-strand-board) or exterior grade plywood at least 12 mm but preferably 18 mm thick, or even better, invest in a purpose-made cement fibreboard that is totally happy about being wet.

Second, bed a stonecast shower tray on sand and cement mortar to level it and give it a secure base. Replace or cover the flooring under it with OSB or plywood, which is stronger and will fare better than moisture-resistant chipboard, again, the thicker the better.

Third, consider using pre-formed acrylic shower panels instead of wall tiles. That way you only have the corner joints to worry about.

Finally, give some thought to the fact that a power shower simulates the condition of wind-driven rain and will help to push water into the walls as well as you, so use the best-quality silicone mastic you can afford to seal the corners. It isn't all the same stuff, even if it looks it, and the price reflects the quality. Mastic needs to be formed as beading about 6 mm wide, and a plastic pointing tool with soapy water will do this neatly. The DIY technique of smearing it into the joint with a spit-covered finger is not quite so effective, but if it makes you happy...

Changing your home's fuel

Many of us will never have the need to think about how our home is fuelled or whether we could improve on it. But for some it is critical. Rural homes away from mains gas may have solid fuel or electric heating that is expensive and inefficient. Installing heating oil or liquid petroleum gas (LPG) systems could pay off in both property value and home economics.

Heating oil

For any home away from mains gas heating, oil is the preferred solution; of the alternatives it has been the cheapest for some time and will probably stay that way until solar energy takes off. As with LPG, the oil needs to be stored on-site in tanks, which totally fail to complement your home and need to be sited carefully.

Oil-storage tanks that are close to boundaries or the windows of your home should have firewalls, if not an actual masonry boundary wall itself; since a firewall has to extend beyond the sides and the top of the tank, it makes sense to build a boundary wall that can offer the needed fire protection as well. The base also has to be slightly oversized for the tank. I have seen tanks installed on concrete and blockwork walls at a very slight gradient (about 5°), which I'm told is just enough to keep them desludged and provides a tiny reserve of fuel if you've left it too late to re-order. Don't be tempted to do the same: using the best-quality heating oil is the best solution, and tanks shouldn't be moved when supplies get low. Farmers seem to run everything from low-grade oil, from their tractors to their heating – a modern oil boiler is packed with energy-efficient, clean-burning technology that won't appreciate this.

Installers of oil appliances and tanks can choose to be registered with OFTEC, the designated 'competent persons' association for this fuel. Members carry ID cards to present themselves and qualify their registration. Commissioning engineers, boiler installers and tank installers are separate registrations that require individuals being qualified in these 'specialities', and I'm sure they will expand even further. The training and registration business seems to be a lucrative one.

The significance of registration enables specialists to do work that by itself would normally warrant a Building Regulation Application, but in their case this can be self-certified. They will also issue you with a certificate of commissioning, without which the boiler may not be covered by the manufacturer's warranty. These certificates are normally provided by the boiler manufacturer.

A separate Benchmark Certificate, which relates to the entire heating and hot-water system, should also be obtained and jointly completed by the installing and commissioning engineer. Part of this certificate says that the installer has shown you how to operate the boiler and the controls, so make sure they have. An example of the Benchmark Certificate for an oil-fired installation is shown opposite; a different one is available for gas.

Fire valves

One of the most important safety features of an oil tank or boiler installation is the remote sensing fire valve that isolates the supply if a fire is detected in the appliance. The valve is fitted to the oil supply pipe outside the building, but with a fire detector inside the boiler casing itself. There is no limit to the extent of the fire detector's remoteness, since if it isn't connected by a line, wireless versions are available, so do not be dissuaded from installing this essential precaution. Wireless models might be the better option if you are concerned about the wire being damaged; wire ones tend to look a bit Heath Robinson, and because they are installed near ground level, anything you can do to protect them is worth it.

For all the benefits of heating oil as a fuel, with a giant green plastic tank stood on bricks in your garden, a fuel line running from it to the home and a valve stuck on the wall, they can look a bit industrial. You can use hard

benchmark

The code of practice for the installation, commissioning & servicing of oil central heating

Installation, Commissioning and Service Record Log Book

CUSTOMER DETAILS

NAME

ADDRESS

TEL No

IMPORTANT

1. Please keep the Log Book in a safe place for future reference.
2. This Log Book is to be completed in full by the competent person(s) who commissioned the boiler and associated equipment and then handed to the customer. When this is done, the Log Book is a commissioning certificate that can be accepted as evidence of compliance with the appropriate Building Regulations.
3. Failure to install and commission this appliance to the manufacturer's instructions may invalidate the warranty.

The above does not affect your statutory rights.

The content of this Log Book has been produced in consultation with

© CENTRAL HEATING INFORMATION COUNCIL

INSTALLER & COMMISSIONING ENGINEER DETAILS

INSTALLER DETAILS

COMPANY NAME	INSTALLATION DATE
ADDRESS	

TECHNICIAN'S NAME	TEL No.
OFTEC REG No. (if applicable)	

COMMISSIONING ENGINEER (IF DIFFERENT)

NAME	COMMISSIONING DATE
ADDRESS	

	TEL No.
OFTEC REG No. (if applicable)	

APPLIANCE, INSTALLATION & CONTROLS DETAILS

CENTRAL HEATING APPLIANCE

MAKE AND MODEL

APPLIANCE SERIAL No.	SEDBUK No.

LOCATION

NEW SYSTEM ☐ or REPLACEMENT ☐

FLUE TYPE

CONVENTIONAL ☐ BALANCED ☐ LOW LEVEL DISCHARGE ☐

➤ NEW SYSTEM ☐ or RE-USE EXISTING ☐

OIL SYSTEM

TANK CAPACITY Rs. MATERIAL: STEEL ☐ or PLASTIC ☐ BUNDED ☐

TYPE OF INSTALLATION NEW SYSTEM ☐ or REPLACEMENT ☐

FIRE VALVE TYPE LOCATION

FIRE VALVE INSTALLATION NEW SYSTEM ☐ or REPLACEMENT ☐

SUPPLY PIPEWORK NEW SYSTEM ☐ or REPLACEMENT ☐

CONTROLS

To comply with the Building Regulations, each section must have a tick in one or other of the boxes.

REQUIREMENT	MEASURES PROVIDED	
1. TIME AND TEMPERATURE CONTROL TO HEATING	ROOM STAT & PROGRAMMER/TIMER ☐	PROGRAMMABLE ROOMSTAT ☐
2. TIME AND TEMPERATURE CONTROL TO HOT WATER	CYLINDER STAT & PROGRAMMER/TIMER ☐	COMBI BOILER ☐
3. HEATING ZONE VALVES	FITTED ☐	NOT REQUIRED ☐
4. THERMOSTATIC RADIATOR VALVES	FITTED ☐	
5. AUTOMATIC BYPASS TO SYSTEM	FITTED ☐	NOT REQUIRED ☐
6. BOILER INTERLOCK	PROVIDED ☐	

PLEASE FOLLOW THE INSTALLATION AND COMMISSIONING INSTRUCTIONS IN THE INSTALLATION MANUAL SUPPLIED WITH THE EQUIPMENT

COMMISSIONING PROCEDURE INFORMATION

FOR ALL BOILERS

Burner

BURNER TYPE PRESSURE JET ☐ VAPORISING ☐ MAKE	
SMOKE NO CO₂ % NET FLUE GAS TEMP °C	
NET EFFICIENCY % FLUE DRAUGHT mm.WG	
OIL FLOW RATE (VAPORISING ONLY) HIGH FIRE ml/min LOW FIRE ml/min	

Circulation

HAS THE SYSTEM BEEN FLUSHED IN ACCORDANCE WITH THE BOILER MANUFACTURER'S INSTRUCTIONS? YES ☐ NO ☐

WHAT WAS THE CLEANSER USED?

HAS AN INHIBITOR BEEN USED? YES ☐ NO ☐

WHICH INHIBITOR WAS USED?

For the central heating mode, measure and record:

CENTRAL HEATING FLOW TEMPERATURE °C

CENTRAL HEATING RETURN TEMPERATURE °C

FOR COMBINATION BOILERS ONLY

HAS A WATER SCALE REDUCER BEEN FITTED? YES ☐ NO ☐

TYPE FITTED?

For the domestic hot water mode, measure and record:

MAXIMUM OPERATING WATER PRESSURE bar

COLD WATER INLET TEMPERATURE °C

HOT WATER OUTLET TEMPERATURE °C

WATER FLOW RATE AT MAXIMUM SETTING lts/min

FOR CONDENSING BOILERS ONLY

HAS THE CONDENSATE DRAIN BEEN INSTALLED IN ACCORDANCE WITH THE MANUFACTURER'S INSTRUCTIONS? YES ☐ NO ☐

FOR ALL INSTALLATIONS

DOES THE HEATING AND HOT WATER SYSTEM COMPLY WITH THE APPROPRIATE BUILDING REGULATIONS? YES ☐

HAS BOILER AND ASSOCIATED EQUIPMENT BEEN INSTALLED AND COMMISSIONED IN ACCORDANCE WITH THE MANUFACTURER'S INSTRUCTIONS? YES ☐

HAVE YOU DEMONSTRATED THE OPERATION OF THE BOILER AND SYSTEM CONTROLS TO THE CUSTOMER? YES ☐

HAVE YOU LEFT ALL THE MANUFACTURER'S LITERATURE WITH THE CUSTOMER? YES ☐

COMPETENT PERSON'S SIGNATURE	CUSTOMER'S SIGNATURE

(To confirm demonstrations of equipment and receipt of appliance instructions)

SERVICE INTERVAL RECORD

It is recommended that your heating system is serviced regularly and that your service engineer completes the appropriate Service Interval Record below.

SERVICE PROVIDER

Before completing the appropriate Service Interval Record below, please ensure you have carried out the service as described in the boiler manufacturer's instructions. Always use the appliance manufacturer's specified spare part when replacing all controls.

SERVICE 1 DATE:	SERVICE 2 DATE:
ENGINEER NAME	ENGINEER NAME
COMPANY NAME	COMPANY NAME
TEL No.	TEL No.
COMMENTS	COMMENTS
SIGNATURE	SIGNATURE
SERVICE 3 DATE:	SERVICE 4 DATE:
ENGINEER NAME	ENGINEER NAME
COMPANY NAME	COMPANY NAME
TEL No.	TEL No.
COMMENTS	COMMENTS
SIGNATURE	SIGNATURE
SERVICE 5 DATE:	SERVICE 6 DATE:
ENGINEER NAME	ENGINEER NAME
COMPANY NAME	COMPANY NAME
TEL No.	TEL No.
COMMENTS	COMMENTS
SIGNATURE	SIGNATURE
SERVICE 7 DATE:	SERVICE 8 DATE:
ENGINEER NAME	ENGINEER NAME
COMPANY NAME	COMPANY NAME
TEL No.	TEL No.
COMMENTS	COMMENTS
SIGNATURE	SIGNATURE
SERVICE 9 DATE:	SERVICE 10 DATE:
ENGINEER NAME	ENGINEER NAME
COMPANY NAME	COMPANY NAME
TEL No.	TEL No.
COMMENTS	COMMENTS
SIGNATURE	SIGNATURE

When all of the above services have been completed, please contact your Service Engineer for an additional service interval record sheet.

---

landscaping to conceal them, but access is important and they can't be sited near to boundaries or doors and windows without fireproof protection; in my opinion, not enough people use the sub-ground tank solution.

You might know LPG as red bottles that appear in chained rows stood against the walls of remote cottages called 'The Hermitage'. Not an attractive proposition, but LPG can be housed in underground tanks out of sight, a much better alternative. The siting of the tank needs to be both discreet and accessible, because the tankers that will deliver your gas need to be able to get within 25 m of it.

Replacing boilers

By far the biggest proportion of new boilers fitted have balanced flues. Technology again is responsible. It used to be the case that you could only fit flues on an external wall to run the short flue pipe through. Now they can be extended for a few metres horizontally to a wall or vertically through the roof, and this has opened up the choice of locations to most rooms of the home. It should be possible to replace an old open-flue boiler with a new balanced-flue one utilising the same flue path through the structure. The benefit of this type of boiler is that air vents are not needed to supply combustion ventilation. Instead, double-walled flues no more than 100 mm in diameter suck in combustion air through the outer tub and push out the exhaust gas through the inner, making them room-sealed. No extractor fan will affect them, so they can be installed in kitchens or bathrooms where fans exist.

Condensing boilers with built-in heat exchangers are the most efficient of all, receiving the top banding (A) in this respect (see below). The exchangers are made from rust-proof material, which means that flue gases are able to cool and condense on the surface without causing any damage. The lower temperature means that they can even have plastic flue pipes. The condensed gas is then discharged via a condensing pipe run to the outside. This pipe must be kept clear at all times. Non-condensing boilers have to run at much higher temperatures to avoid this condensation, which would normally cause corrosion, and by doing so they are less efficient.

If you choose a condensing boiler, the way you run it will affect its efficiency to some extent, but probably not enough to worry about it. Running it with lower return water temperature and heating large radiators will keep it operating in condensing mode. These efficiencies are measured as a percentage, with A being somewhere between 90 and 94 per cent, and G being somewhere between 50 and 70 per cent. D is the minimum allowed for new boilers in dwellings under the Building Regulations 2000. The scheme is apparently only temporary until such times as a European directive for labelling is introduced.

Technology seems to be improving all the time, and certainly some of these boilers are being produced much smaller than before, with the intention of being housed in kitchen units. You have some restrictions in locating these, due to the condensate drain (which can be long but still has to have a fall to the outside) and the expansion relief outlet, which has the ability to purge hot water from it and shouldn't be located above head height. Over doorways is not good: even if the pipe is turned back into the wall to receive the water, it will damage your brickwork, if not your head.

Once again, you need to find a CORGI- or OFTEC-registered installer for these products, depending on whether they are gas- or oil-fired.

Combi boilers

When they first appeared, combis seemed only to fill a specific niche in the market: flats. Why else would you buy an expensive and complicated package of a boiler that could run the heating and hot water supply without all the gubbins in the attic, unless it was because you didn't have an attic? Even with improved technology, reduced size and better flow rates, combis still only get fitted in new flats and not new houses.

The drawback with combis is the flow rate, which isn't enough. Ten litres per minute on average is no good for family use. Running a bath takes time with a combi, quite a long time – and if somebody elsewhere turns a tap on, it might never happen. High-flow ones can reach 15 l per minute, which is just about the bottom line of acceptable in my eyes.

I mention combis here because they find a new niche in renovation work. A combi boiler can give you space for something else, whether it is the potential for a future loft conversion or the chance to remodel the bathroom minus the airing cupboard plumbing. I know airing cupboards are useful, but you can heat any cupboard with a bit of hot water pipe, and losing the storage cylinder, pump, diverter valves and all the other array of copperware that goes with vented systems can be very liberating. You could convert an airing cupboard to a shower – in a post-1960s home, it might be the only place where you can fit a shower, apart from in the bath.

Combis come under the heading of sealed systems, which means they aren't open-vented and contain an expansion vessel for dealing with the expanded volume of water when it heats up. The vessel has to cope with the expansion that would occur from a 10°C increase in water temperature up to 100°C. To run at all, they must be charged with an adequate amount of water pressure, usually around 1 bar, and they tend to stop running altogether when the pressure drops below the minimum.

If the pressure drops the system must be topped up by way of a filling loop. A flexible pipe is either plumbed in with it, or you can attach and detach a valve, open it and charge the system to its optimum running pressure. Since water in a sealed system should not evaporate, you can only get air in and hence reduced pressure after refilling it with water, so the pressure shouldn't be dropping in any other circumstance. If it does, you might have a leak – check your radiator valves and the like. This lack of air in a sealed system comes with some hidden benefits: corrosion should all but be eliminated, and because you don't have water tanks and pipes in the loft, you will have less condensation up there.

You don't have to have a combi boiler to have a sealed system; all the components squashed inside a combi can be located outside with a large, unvented hot-water cylinder that stores plenty of hot water.

Unvented hot-water cylinders

Unlike conventional open-vented hot-water cylinders that take their water from a cold water tank in the loft, unvented ones take it directly off the mains. No water tanks are required, which is the primary reason why they are becoming popular in the UK now, even though they have been around on the Continent for some time. They are especially good for running showers, given their pressure balance with the mains supply. Since their introduction, however, they have been covered by the Building Regulations because of their inherent safety requirements – incorrectly installed, you more or less have the potential for a hot-water bomb. Qualified installers are essential for these, and the cylinder itself needs to be approved by the British Board of Agrement.

Cylinders have been available here since the late 1980s but have only become popular since the turn of the century. You have the choice of heating them directly off an immersion heater if you wish, but most are indirectly heated by your boiler. With the pressure and temperature of the supply maintained, even when other taps draw off water,

they are provided in preference to most combi boilers. They are lined with glass, stainless steel or copper.

Receiving hot water direct from the boiler means a faster response to providing hot water, which is why they are so popular; that, and their large store of hot water. In models fitted with a return loop and pump, mains-pressure hot water can be delivered. The cylinders can sometimes be used with condensing boilers for added efficiency.

Like combis, unvented cylinders provide hot water without the need for a cold-water storage tank in the loft. Traditional indirect heating systems heated the water rather slowly with a coil, but these cylinders are directly connected to the primary heating circuit. The heat is passed to the cold water mains through an efficient heat exchanger, and high flow rates can be achieved. When you look at the 10 l per minute from a combi, the flow rate here can be twice or three times that. If you have two mixer showers to feed, you will really need that 30 l per minute flow rate. This is the kind of water supply that will keep a family happy, but to house it you need a family-sized space.

Garages and roof spaces are viable options, but you might try building a cupboard around the cylinder if you have to have it in the home. Sizes range from 100 to 500 l capacity, but they all look capacious to me. This can be a bit of a major drawback in an existing home that's tight on space. Kitchens are not so good, as you may want the space for something else; I have seen cylinders occupy the entire 2 m-high larder cupboard in a flat, leaving nowhere for food storage. And if you can't help but install one in a bedroom, the heat from it will make the room unusable in summer.

Technical restrictions

Cylinders can be used to provide space-heating water in addition to hot tap water, and in this instance they are referred to as integrated thermal stores. There are a few questions to be asked before you decide – is my mains water supply able to serve it? Is the pressure coming into the home high enough, and is the flow rate sufficient? If it isn't, your cylinder may prove expensively inadequate.

Make sure your installer takes a pressure reading and a flow rate reading when he prices the job, and decide on that basis whether to proceed. Plenty of us suffer from low water pressure, and with the increase in development, water will be subjected to higher demand in the future. In areas of high demand, authorities may only have to provide minimum standards of pressure and flow to your home, and these may well be woefully short of your needs. In an older property, you might have to consider replacing the mains supply from the boundary stopcock – this is the section of water pipe feeding your home, for which you have responsibility (as opposed to the water company), and that could be a lot of pipe and expense.

If you're adding bathroom facilities to your home, consider this: a main bathroom with shower and bath, plus an en-suite shower room and a downstairs WC, in other words the standard arrangement for family homes now, can be demanding on water flow. Two showers might need 14 l per minute each, and both running together could be asking a lot from the supply pipe; even though a pressure of 3 bar or so might be there, the flow rate could be nowhere near enough. End result, one of the showers runs at a trickle, if at all.

Unvented cylinders need at least 1 bar of supply pressure but also at least 20 l per minute flow rate; add up your household demands for flow and see what you need. Some cylinders come with an additional accumulator vessel attached that that holds the cold water at mains pressure and feeds the unvented cylinder. This helps to increase the flow rate in the system, balancing the flow at the taps and letting you run multiple taps and showers together.

Because unvented systems fed direct by mains water supply are pressurised, they come complete with safety devices packaged in and can only be installed by a registered operative, licensed to install or commission them: you might find it impossible to have it commissioned if you have had an unregistered installer put it in. It's important that you see and validate the operative's identity card, which should confirm whether they are specifically qualified to install this type of system. Generalised institute membership cards and the like are no substitute.

CHAPTER SIX

Refitting and Refinishing

REFINISHING OUTSIDE
Stonework

To my eye, nothing looks finer in a house wall than stonework, but apparently this isn't a very Anglo-Saxon thing. The Romans introduced us to the skills of quarrying and cutting stone for building, and we let them get on with it until they left. Nobody bothered after that until the Normans turned up and started building churches everywhere. The Normans

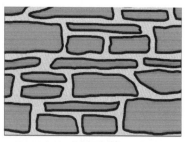
Slate walling

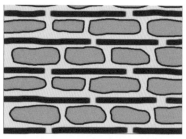
Boulder and slate walling

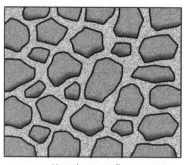
Kentish rag walling

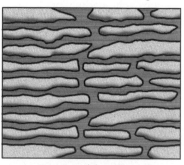
Limestone slab walling

Yorkshire Pennines millstone grit

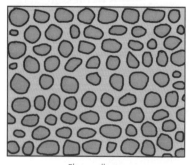
Flint walling

Vernacular stone.

loved building with stone, and this time some of that enthusiasm must have rubbed off because the noble art of a stonemason stayed and enjoyed considerable status in our society.

Vernacular stonework

Stone tends to have been used indigenously in building for obvious reasons: it cost a lot to transport it, so if it wasn't available locally it wasn't available. In Yorkshire it is Pennine millstone, in Derbyshire limestone, in Cornwall it's granite or slate, and in Kent, it's ragstone. Even hard chalk has been used cut into blocks, known as clunch, particularly in Hampshire and Sussex, but it proved not to be a great success due to its poor weathering ability and tendency to absorb damp.

Flints are also common in construction in the east and southeast of England, where they occur naturally

Rubble wall

Sold stone

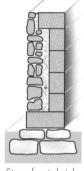

Stone-front, brick-backed wall

Watershot stone wall

Methods of stone walling.

Uncoursed random rubble

Coursed random rubble

Random rubble brought to course

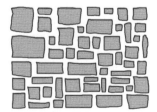

Squared random rubble uncoursed

Squared random rubble coursed

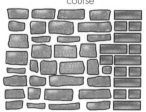

Uncoursed stone in conjunction with brick

Styles of stonework.

121

in chalk beds. Flint is hardness itself and doesn't wear at all, making it an excellent wall-building material if it wasn't for one other characteristic – it takes a highly amorphous form that makes it difficult to joint. Shaping or napping flints, so they can be tightly fitted together in lime mortar, is a skill that is virtually extinct. The flintwork we see in buildings today looks more like rendering pebble-dashed with flint than anything else. You have only to look at a flint wall built 100 years ago to see the difference, but you have to sympathise with the mason. The surface of flint is smooth and impervious, unlike the other stones and unlike brick, so it has no key to bond the mortar to.

Flint can be laid coursed, uncoursed or rough-coursed. The hard work of masons in the past in knapping and even squaring flints individually enabled them to be laid in straight rows tightly fitting together. Knapping is basically whacking the flint to split it in two (fairly easy, as flint is so brittle), exposing a black polished centre that can be used to face the wall. Not all flints have a black core; some tend towards blue or grey-blue shades and some are speckled with white, so if you are repairing or infilling a knapped flint wall you may need to source the flints to blend as well as match the coursing style. Flint-knapping is an old craft that can be dated back to around 1300, but it wasn't until the mid-18th century that squaring and coursing flintwork became popular. Flint walls often fail by bowing out because of the fact that the material is relatively

thin once knapped and doesn't bond into a reasonable thickness for stability. Builders have tried to overcome this by using it between brick or stone quoins or in lacing courses, but it can still be a problem over time. A flint wall needs to be 450 mm thick to have inherent strength, or at the very least 338 mm between quoins – and many aren't anywhere near this.

In East Anglia, it became popular in churches to use inset panels of chequerwork with flints carefully cut and shaped set in lime mortar. The stone was cut to fit in a square pocket and a pattern like a mosaic of decoration was formed. You could do worse than introduce your own flint chequerwork pattern to an old stone wall, but make sure it is thick enough to start with.

In the last decade of the 20th century flint blocks became available which took some of the hard work out of building with flints. Knapped and set in moulds the blocks are concrete-poured with the flints proud of the surface, waiting to be pointed up in situ. If done well, pointing does conceal the shape of the blockwork, but not completely, and you end up with a mixture of uncoursed walling in squares. The problem is that all too often I've seen it done badly – I'm sure it's possible to reach an unacceptable appearance using flints if enough care is taken with the pointing.

In some northern areas stones are laid at a rakish angle to resist the penetration of wind-driven rain. This technique, known as 'watershot', is

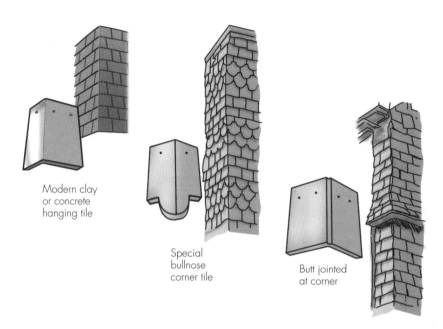

Modern clay
or concrete
hanging tile

Special
bullnose
corner tile

Butt jointed
at corner

The changing corners of tile hanging.

seen in the Lake District and Pennines. The mortar joints are recessed and pointed, and are set some 50 mm back into the face of the stonework to allow the water to run off without absorption into the joints.

The style stonework takes on is dependent on the nature of the stone itself. When it's quarried, it breaks and splits according to its nature, and the shape of the final cut stones reflects this. Slate walling, for example, comprises a variety of shapes from thin, elongated slivers bonded over more rectangular sections, and in contrast, Kent ragstone tends to be boulder-like in a polygonal way but quite uniform in shape.

Keeping stonework in the vernacular is important, and it's worth taking time to look around the area before you begin, and see what materials and constructions methods have been used in the past.

Vertical tiling (tile-hanging)

Vertical tiling doesn't have gravity on its side. With modern plain tiles being twice holed and nailed with aluminium nails to battens, the risk of dislodging and slipping over the years is much reduced, but in the past, tile-hanging was often exactly that.

Covering a wall with roof tiles isn't a new concept, but dates back to the end of the 17th century, primarily in the southeast of Britain. Here the vernacular architecture of jettied upper floors was at one time commonly infilled beneath to extend the ground floor. When this was done, the upper floor wall of wattle and daub render could be weathered with vertical tiles to align with the brick infill wall beneath. The hand-made clay tiles of the southeast provided better weather resistance than soft bricks and render, but the fixing was a bit unreliable. Many original tiles don't have nibs to hang off battens; instead, oak pegs were used to hang off riven oak lathes. Peg tiles are particularly common in Kent and Sussex.

Decorative tiles like bullnoses, fishtails and arrowheads were first made in the 18th century, and the practice of adding decorative tile courses to tile hanging is still popular. The style of hanging tiles to mimic brickwork also became popular in the late 17th century and is known as mathematical tiling. Lime mortar was used to bed the tiles in and point between them, as you would bricks, and because of this technique mathematical tiling has survived. The fashion of the era lay towards bricks, and 'mathematical' tiling was a way of giving the appearance of brickwork without the cost of rebuilding.

Because of the way the tiles interlock, repairing mathematical tiling isn't easy and you may have to remove and refix them over a bigger area than you thought. You may have some luck by removing a corner tile and sliding out a row. The oak laths on which they hang may be suffering from rot and need to be replaced.

If you don't mind the transition to modern materials, you might resist the urge to rehang them with wooden pegs and use aluminium nails instead. Be careful to use a soft mix of lime mortar when bedding them in, not cement mortar. Cement mortars are much harder and less permeable, so if rain gets behind the wall, it can only seep out through the tiles and not the mortar joints, which will weaken the tiles quickly.

Plain tiles today tend to have a batten gauge of around 110 mm; with treated softwood battens 38 mm wide and nibs to overhang them, they can be quite durable. Tiles can still become damaged by frost and need to be refixed, and it should be possible to replace them as individuals carefully if you can live without nailing home the odd replacement. Where areas need to be repaired, it's a case of taking them down from the eaves course and nailing the replacements with 38 mm aluminium nails. Don't be over-enthusiastic with the nailing: even new concrete tiles are so fragile that one extra nail blow can crack them. I spent the hottest days of summer hanging tiles, and I can tell you it takes a little practice to judge the amount of hammer blow in the nailing.

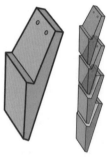

Mathematical tiling.

Be on the lookout for hairline fractures that are scarcely visible when you're nailing but appear when you reach a few courses above, as the tile drops in half. I've learnt that tile hanging takes patience and shade.

REFINISHING INSIDE
Plastering
Refinishing ceilings

Few of us appreciate ceilings – this is a fact that is apparent the moment you walk into some homes. What remains on the ceiling is the last fad. Fads make us do odd things to them from time to time, like sticking polystyrene tiles to them or boarding them over with tongue-and-groove softwood. Coating them in textured plastic paint so a pattern can be dragged through it was the last fad, but most of the time we ignore the ceiling. The prospect of doing any work to a soffit is an unpleasant one, made that way by the mess and the general awkwardness of working upside down. The current trend of a smooth plaster finish is a good one in my book, but I doubt that it will last forever. Plaster ceilings aren't very practical: they crack easily with the shrinkage of new joists and require a skilled craftsman's hand to skim out a perfectly smooth and level finish.

Polystyrene tiles and timber boarding can only be removed or boarded over with plasterboard, but textured paint can be refinished with plaster. Textured paint ('Artex') was with us all the way in the 1970s and 1980s, but since the Millennium, and like most things from that era, it has become an embarrassment. It will probably undergo a revival now I've said that. I always thought that, like the icing on a cake, you could overdo it, and for some coated ceilings the finish has become too much to live with. You don't have to. Armed with a can of PVA bonding to coat the sugar-soaped surface, you can skim over it to a smooth plastered finish. The depth of the Artex finish will have some bearing here on whether you need to apply and undercoat as well as a finishing coat.

Manufacturers tend to recommend that plaster finish coats are kept to 2 or 3 mm thick, so in most cases a bonding undercoat will be needed first. The treatment of a bonding agent to the surface is important to prepare it and form a good key. These solutions are often coloured, so you can see where solution been applied and where it hasn't. Bonding agents are needed where the suction from the surface is too high and simply wetting it first isn't going to be enough.

Matching wall rendering

If rendering has blown away from the wall or cracked beyond hope, hacking it off and reapplying it will be the only solution. The difficulty comes in trying to match it with the original finish. Rough-cast renders (known as harling in some areas) have been very popular in Britain and traditionally consist of slaked lime, sand and stone chippings, which are all mixed together before being applied.

Similar to this, but with added fun for the family, is pebbledash render.

The stone chippings here are thrown in handfuls at the wet render soon after it has been applied to the walls, and with luck some will stick. You don't need to throw them so hard as to bury the little devils, but at the same time you don't want too deep a pile of stones building up on the ground beneath. The stone chippings need to be sourced to match, and can be anything from rounded pea shingle to coarse grit or mineral chippings.

In the early 17th century, decorative smooth rendering became fashionable in timber-framed homes. Given the cost of timber at the time, it was cheaper to use rendered panels in a framework of timber rather than wooden boarding. Known as pargeting, patterns of combing or irregular stick shapes developed and grew in some parts of the country to a highly elaborate peak around the middle of the 17th century. It stayed in vogue for about a hundred years, and it is still possible to see plenty of homes decorated in this style in the southeast and East Anglia.

Render and set

For solid walls some builders won't use anything but a base coat of cement and sand render first. This scratch coat is evenly applied and scored to provide a key for the finishing plaster. Cement and sand is the opposite to lightweight plaster, and it pays to use the best-quality soft sand you can afford. Not all sand is ideal for rendering; some of it (notably that sold nationwide by DIY stores) is fit for concrete mixing but little else. Ask your plasterer for advice on which sand to use if you are buying materials on a labour-only arrangement.

Traditional plastering, using a sand and cement base coat and a finishing plaster topcoat, has to some extent become outmoded. For one thing, the materials of good quality sand and ordinary Portland cement are not cheap, and for another, getting the mix right to avoid it cracking is not that easy. Interior plastering has made a move towards thistle gypsum plasters that need only water and application. Like cement they have a shelf life and can't be bought and stored too far in advance of their use, three or four months at most.

Thistle plaster

A wide variety of thistle plasters are now available, depending on the finish required and the surface you are plastering to. Some are single-coat plasters and others two-coat that need an undercoat application first. All have varying coverage from a 25 kg bag. The table opposite gives some idea of how much you'll need, based on an 11 mm thickness to walls of undercoat and a 2 mm thickness of topcoat. The one-coat system gets 13 mm in one application and has proved popular for applying direct to aerated block inner walls. Ceilings should have a reduced thickness of 8 mm at most.

Replicating historical and decorative plastering

Stucco rendering was popular on the outside of buildings in the late 18th and early 19th centuries. It was

TOPCOATS	Coverage 25 kg bag	Drying time	Background
Renovating finish plaster	10.5 sq m	2 hrs	Replastering
Plaster finish	10.5 sq m	2 hrs	Any undercoat
Board finish	10.5 sq m	1.5 hrs	Plasterboard
Multi-finish	10.5 sq m	1.5 hrs	Multi-purpose
UNDERCOATS			
Renovating	3 sq m	1.5–2 hrs	Replastering
Bonding	2.75 sq m	1.5–2 hrs	Low-suction
Browning	3.5 sq m	1.5–2 hrs	Medium-suction
Universal one-coat	2.25 sq m	1.5–2 hrs	General
Hardwall	3 sq m	1.5–2 hrs	General

intended to imitate stone and designed to be a hard surface that utilised Roman cement to that aim (Portland cement didn't usurp it until the middle of the 19th century) – but inside was different. Lime plasters were eventually used internally because they were soft and flexible, although in the past lime plaster tended to be much coarser in texture than it is today. With refinement it became possible to use smoother lime plasters for decorative and ornate work

Some cornices could be drawn out with a wooden block mould in situ, but other ceiling rose features and the like were formed in moulds and stuck on later – not all, though, because

plasterers had a habit of making their own tools for carving out or impressing plaster before it set in place. Some of the sculptural beauty of plaster features gets lost over time beneath layers of paintwork and chips, but it is possible to restore them to a near original condition.

Plastering restoration specialists use similar methods of dexterity and skill to renovate plasterwork. Missing pieces of plasterwork can be replaced by taking a rubber 'squeeze' of the remaining ornament and casting a new section from the mould, or by 'rerunning' a coving or cornice length. Not all decoration in period homes is plaster, though – some of it could be powdered chalk and linseed oil mixed together as a cheap alternative, or even papier-mâché.

The mix of the plaster in a period home will have been decided upon by the availability of local materials. Sand needed to be good-quality and not salty or silty; animal by-products used in the mix might vary from horse or goat hair to cow dung and even blood, and other binding agents included cheese and straw chopped up into fine pieces.

Most of the art went out of plasterwork after the Edwardian era, but now that plaster has taken back over from plastic paint, decorative plasterwork for ceilings is becoming popular once again. Handmade ornate panels and mouldings in cast form appear to be a bit rough when they are first stuck in place. Be patient: with careful finishing the blemishes should be filled and lost when the plasterer is complete. Finding the right setting for a decorative plaster ceiling in a modern home is not so easy. If you do have a high enough ceiling level to achieve it, getting the accent lighting right to display it will be important. The last plaster art ceiling I saw, panelled and embossed with raised Tudor roses, had every rose centre cut out and a recessed halogen spot lamp set in place where it had been. Taste had definitely left the building.

Refitting kitchens
Styles
It seems that a kitchen refit is still an essential part of most renovation projects. We change our kitchens almost as frequently as we redecorate now. If it isn't a complete removal and replacement that you want, you can improve what you have by fitting new doors to the cupboards and changing the handles. In TV-land when DIY shows knock on your door you can always expect to find your kitchen looking unrecognisable before they leave, whether it be with sticky-back plastic or a new state-of-the-art stainless-steel fit-out. Two things are obvious: one, you can pay what you like to renovate a kitchen, and two, whatever you do, the chances are that the next owner of the home will hate it. Personal taste rules in this room more than any other. In my opinion a kitchen style that reflects the home's architecture is an appropriate one.

Stainless steel is popular in 2004, which is odd because not ten years ago it was considered to be the cheap look for a sink and drainer. White-coated stonecast was the quality sink then, all of which goes to show that with kitchens you should avoid fashion like the plague and fit one that suits you and your home. Trends will come and go, and you may spend a small fortune on the current vogue, only to find that you joined the fashion stakes just as it was about to leave – which is yet another reason for choosing a style of kitchen that reflects the architecture of your home.

In a contemporary home, the commercial look of stainless steel or the quality of cast glass may be a timeless solution. Ditto the natural oak finish in a country farmhouse, which always looks like it belongs with the

Planning a kitchen.

property and is always in context. White is also a choice for longevity, in particular when your kitchen is not blessed with a wealth of daylight or your home has no particular architectural style.

The style choice

If you're not troubled by bringing continuity to your home through its architecture, and linking the interior with the exterior design seems an unnecessary restriction, you have a wealth of kitchen styles to choose from. I'm not about to describe all of them here, but what follows is a selection pack of the most popular in their purist form. It is of course common practice to mix these styles to whatever end you or your kitchen fitters see fit, and hybrid styles are just as popular. The contemporary farmhouse, the Victorian minimalist and so on will magnify out the choices even more.

Farmhouse

Farmhouse or country kitchens are timeless favourites, with an air of healthy rustic living about them. Real timber doors in natural pine or a limed appearance are standard. It is possible to paint the doors and still hold the look, but it helps if the paintwork is distressed, giving it a well-worn charm. The style suits tiled or blocked-wood worktops, terracotta quarry-tiled floors and wooden windows. With dark wood units it helps if your kitchen has a bountiful supply of daylight.

Farmhouse kitchens are often blocks of fittings in square and chunky dimensions, and seem to like being cluttered with furniture, with pots and pans on display along with crockery in plate racks. Everything that can be nailed to the wall often is. Slot-in or free-standing white goods rather than built-in are the order of the day, and porcelain butler sinks help a lot with the square and chunky look. A free-standing pine Welsh dresser seems to be essential.

Shaker

The Shakers were of the opinion that the kitchen should be, and should appear to be a hub of calmness and efficiency bathed in cool colours. The doors are simplistic but stylish, with clean lines and square edges that aren't cluttered by decoration or arty bits. When you look at a Shaker kitchen it calms you – it says hey, no fancy tricks

here, everything is nice and easy, just where you need it to be; functional. Natural-wood worktops and smooth panelled door fronts can be painted in calming pastel or muted colours. You can convert any kitchen to Shaker style by changing the doors and taking out the gadgets. Doors can easily be made up from MDF, primed and painted to a smooth eggshell or matt finish. The style can look very 1950s and similar to Retro.

Retro

The style of the 1950s differs from Shaker in one important way: the edges are all rounded instead of being square-cut. Soft curves go with clean lines and a lino or vinyl floor covering. Chequered floor coverings and flowery curtains are essential elements in any retro kitchen. Worktops would be Formica if it wasn't for the fact that melamine has replaced it, but you can find a suitable finish in a bold colour and shiny choice. Stainless-steel appliances are a must, and if you can add some bright and invasive primary colours to the walls and a vinyl-covered bar stool, they will complete the picture.

Classic

In some form or another, classic kitchens are by far the most popular. They look great in white or light wood finishes like beech and maple. The door fronts and trims have just enough architecture in them to make them interesting without being over the top. Classic kitchens are in the affordable range of laminated MDF doors as well as natural wood. Curved panels and glass door display units help to make the classic look, and the fun really starts with the accessories. Any high-quality worktop will work, but equally so will a melamine-faced chipboard one.

Contemporary

Modernism in its most up-to-date form, contemporary design is simple and stylish. with the added bonus of a look of quality and expense. Materials of choice are glass, stainless steel, stone floors, polished stone worktops and glass splashback tiles. The stainless-steel cooker extractor hobs that appeared around the Millennium are at the centre of contemporary design. White goods and accessories are mostly built in and hidden, unless they have glass fronts and blend in with the futuristic look. Minimalism could be described as contemporary without the knobs on – literally.

The worktop choice
Laminated chipboard

The base material of the worktop world is 25 mm-thick chipboard covered by melamine, which seems to come in a never-ending range of patterns and colours to suit any kitchen. It is damageable, though, by being scratched or melting beneath hot pans, so worktop savers are needed to avoid accidents. If you do damage the surface, water will be able to get under the melamine finish and cause it to bubble up in an irreparable manner. For exposed ends of worktop, iron-on strips are available, but it is possible to

end up with a lot of waste in this material which is purchased off the shelf in 3 m lengths. Mitred joining can be done at the corners flawlessly by skilled fitters, and most kitchen-fit companies have one or two individuals who join the worktop to perfection.

Granite

A stone worktop may seem like a statement of wealth in a 'look what we've spent on the kitchen refit' kind of way, but in fact it has great practical benefits. Of the natural stones, granite is the hardest-wearing and perhaps most easily maintained material. It might just be possible to scratch it if you try hard enough, but in general the polished surface has a diamond-hard quality about it. The colour of granite varies from stylish charcoal blacks to almost pale terracotta. It must be a workable material because drainers are commonly honed out of it, and in bathroom furnishings, vanity unit tops with the bowls are made out a single block of stone.

If you plan to order granite worktops, you are going to have to become a perfectionist when it comes to checking the installation. Make sure that the corners are seamlessly joined together and are finished perfectly at the edges. Stone is exacting, and if you're paying that kind of money for it you want it to be right and look right. How else can you tell people what you've spent on it ?

Corian

Invented in the 1970s, this was the first man-made product to combine natural minerals with pigments and a pure acrylic polymer. The product is incredibly versatile and used in many industries for all kinds of products. Corian worktops can be made to measure, so careful measuring is essential when planning.

Luxore

Not a luxury hotel on the Las Vegas Strip, but a quartz-based man-made material that chooses appearance over hardness. It has a crystalline finish that sparkles when lit. Luxore is produced in colours that aren't available in natural stone – vivid reds and blues as well as more conventional colours, and the finish is as high-gloss as you can get. To my mind, it is more suited to fitted bathrooms than to kitchens.

Caesarstone

Yet another of the man-made products, this combines quartz and crushed aggregates with pigments and polymers. It is said to make granite look soft, being almost five times harder. Like Corian, it has the advantage of being free from imperfections and is produced to order, including the colour. This would be the bee's knees in designer kitchen worktops for those people who need total colour control or who just can't bear the imperfections and inconsistancies of natural granite.

Stainless steel

New to the domestic market around the turn of the last century, stainless steel is the favoured material in commercial kitchens. It can look a little sterile, and careful décor and lighting are needed to soften its appearance. Choose fluorescent under-unit worktop lights, for example, instead of ceiling spots that have a tendency to produce too much glare from the surface.

Glass

Glass is a favourite material for me, so I'm slightly biased here. Made to order by companies who specialise in cast glass furnishings, it creates an original and functional worktop. Heat-resistant and easy to clean, it is the only worktop material that can be lit from below. Due to its thickness, which is greater than with the other materials, its exposed edges have a depth of greenness to them that needs to co-ordinate with the colour scheme in the room – not even clear cast glass is 'clear'. That isn't a problem, and using glass tiles for a splashback complements it perfectly. If glass has a drawback, it is that being cast does mean it has imperfections, bubbles for example, but it is all the more beautiful for them.

The sink choice
Belfast sinks

The style of sink you choose will, in some part at least, be determined by the style of the units and worktop. The classic Belfast sinks of vitrified clay became the in thing in the late 1990s, but for them to look the part, a wood-block worktop and a Victorian-style kitchen, taps and all, is really needed. Trying to get a Belfast sink to look right in a classic kitchen is always

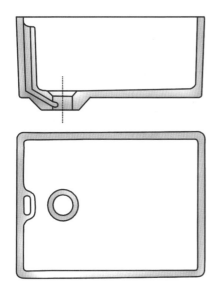

Belfast sink.

so the benefit of having a really deep and large sink is lost on us. QED: the only reason for fitting one is design, which brings me full circle around to my first point.

Stainless steel

For sinks this material left us in the 1980s – but not for long – in 2004 it's back at the height of popularity. On a practical level 18/10 chrome nickel steel (stainless steel to you and I) is considered to be the durable and hygienic solution. It all looks the same, but apparently some of it is finished with a texturing anti-scratch surface that also complements aluminium appliances, which is why it is popular in the contemporary style of kitchen.

going to be like pushing an elephant up the stairs (at some point you are going to stop and wonder why you're doing it). In the 21st century a lot of us don't bathe our small children in the kitchen sink, any more than we wash our clothes or even our crockery in it,

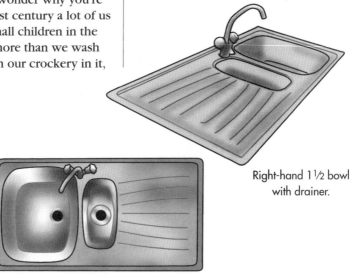

Right-hand 1 ½ bowl with drainer.

Left-hand 1 ½ bowl with drainer.

Ceramic

Ceramic or stone-cast sinks are always a good choice for kitchens. Made from versatile materials that blend in with pretty much any kitchen style. Because they are kiln-fired under extremely high temperatures, nothing in the way of hot pans is going to touch them, and the choice of a textured or smooth polished finish is yours. A wide range of colours in sinks is not really available yet (if it ever will be), but ceramic always looks best in white, the only problem being finding white waste fittings to match them. Plastic plug holes aren't made now (presumably because they crack and aren't at all durable), so if you buy a white sink it will probably come with a stainless steel plug hole. Having a stainless steel plug hole means having to have chrome taps instead of white – and before you know it, you want a stainless-steel sink.

Plastic

At the lower end of the market are plastic sinks, which are as lightweight and durable as plastic shower trays, but without adjustable feet. The dilemma of the white sink is covered under ceramic above.

Fragranite

Another hybrid material for you to wrestle with, fragranite, as you've no doubt guessed, has some granite in it – in fact, about 80 per cent is granite particles that afford it strength, durability and scratch resistance. Able to resist temperatures up to 280°C, which should just about cope with hot pans but not actual fire, it can come as polished smooth or textured.

Integral stone sinks

One of the great advantages of having a worktop honed from a single piece of stone such as limestone or granite is that the sink bowl can also be cut from it as one homogenous lump. I've made that sound so attractive, but these sink bowls have a natural free-form look that has to be the very best appearance money can buy.

Perhaps the real choice with sinks is the drainer choice – single or double. If it's single, then left-hand or right-hand bowl – and then having cleared that hurdle, you can move straight on to the material choice, passing Go and collecting £200 on the way.

Practical kitchens

I should have put this section ahead of the kitchen styles one, but since that was the fun part, the urge to get to it would have been too much for many of you to bear. Now, having decided on the style, it's time to consider the practicalities of kitchen design. You can work through your practical needs for this room in three key parts.

Function

Assessing the function of your kitchen means looking in detail at how you plan to use it and how many people will use the room. Will children or seniors be using it as well? Apart from cooking and the type of cooking you do (eg microwave, oven-ready, baking or gourmet?), what other functions will the kitchen have to serve –

laundry room, cleaner's cupboard, breakfasting space etc?

Use

The use of your kitchen takes the function one step further, and you should look at whether you plan to use the room to entertain guests in or from, or indeed whether you plan to watch TV or listen to the radio or hi-fi while working there.

Storage

Storage requirements are best looked at against an inventory of your needs. Crockery, cutlery, food, cooking pots and pans, glasses, trays – the wealth of differently shaped objects is always the problem. Some of these things just aren't easy to store. How you do your shopping will also decide how much food storage space you need – likewise whether you recycle any waste products. I could quote you the basic minimum volumes for storage space in new homes, but you would laugh your way through the rest of this chapter.

Practical design

Having your kitchen designed for free by installers is one way forward, and without a doubt it is worth having their advice in this area. I wouldn't, however, rely upon it completely; you need to guide them, rather than letting them guide you. This will be your kitchen, and giving plenty of thought now to your options will pay off.

Start by measuring up the room, and prepare a scale plan of the room with all the exterior walls marked and coloured. The external walls are everything to kitchen design – daylight, ventilation, drainage, extractors, water etc. The more outside walls you have, the greater flexibility you have over where things go. Next, mark in the services that exist at present and their position: gas, water, power points. All of these can be extended, but there are limitations.

With this done, you can decide on what appliances you want and whether you have the room to get them all in. Storage space is just as important, but if it comes to it, reducing the volume of storage can be acceptable to fit in a dishwasher. Many years ago, when domestic engineering received government advice, the ideal arrangement of the cooker, fridge and sink in a kitchen was drawn by a triangle of minimum and maximum sides. The efficiency triangle, as it was known, is still used today, but although the theory is not bad the dimension of the sides (between 3.3 and 6.6 m) is too big for many homes. And unless you're a celebrity chef cooking for dinner parties daily, you'll want, as everybody does, the kitchen to look nice first and work efficiently second. Labour-saving devices have taken much of the effort out of kitchen work, and having an 'inefficient triangle' is no longer likely to hospitalise you.

The other point about ergonomics is that it turns out that the perfect kitchen shape is circular – but how many round kitchens do you see? Fitting a circular work zone into a rectangular kitchen is a waste of space that most of us can ill afford; unless you are remodelling the inside walls, in which case you could build curved partitions, you'll be stuck with the square like the rest of us.

You almost certainly don't have the space for everything you'd like, which should help you focus on what your needs really are. Technology is helping all the time when it comes to space-saving solutions. Tumble-dryers that condense the water vapour internally and require no external vents can be located anywhere there is a power point: an understair cupboard, for example. Built-in fridges and ovens come in a variety of sizes that will fit out a caravan-sized flat or an executive home. You can even buy a mini fitted kitchen that occupies no more space than a standard sink unit. Designed for bedsits, office tea-rooms and the like, it consists of a single drainer sink attached to an electric hob with a fridge and microwave beneath, all built into a single unit and with an efficiency triangle absolutely nowhere to be seen. There really isn't a minimum size for a kitchen, it's down to your individual needs – but if you want it to enhance the value of your home, it should reflect your home's size.

Deciding where the kitchen sink goes is a good place to start – usually because there aren't that many options. Sinks need some daylight, and we traditionally locate the sink under the window so that the domestic engineer can look out while doing the washing-up and ponder over the meaning of life or what the postman has in his sack today.

Dishwashers have made things a little different, but daylight and sinks are still good companions, and should be kept together.

It's all the more surprising, then, that more people don't install kitchen lighting to spotlight down over the sink. Directing it in from the centre of the ceiling can mean you have to stand in your own shadow, so think about the relationship between the sink and lighting. I have seen kitchen ceilings peppered with low-voltage halogens, looking like a barn door in a shotgun blast, but still somehow failing to light over the sink. With kitchen wall units either side you should be able to carry a light plinth over the sink that can house recessed halogens. The top of the units should frame the window head so that the window isn't hindered. Alternatives to creating 'light bridges' like this come in the form of cable lighting kits that stretch taut wires for spots to connect to between walls or units.

Kitchen stoves and ranges

For those who want to roast a whole pig or heat the house with the kitchen stove, here is some invaluable, if not empathetic advice. If you are planning to install any kind of stove that relies on an open flue, you are going to need to bring air to the room you install it in. This air is not for you to breathe under the wall of heat, but for combustion: it will ensure that the appliance stays lit and the flue gases go out through the flue. Flue gases contain carbon monoxide, which you don't want spilling out into the room.

The risk of gas spillage occurring is higher than you might think, because we have grown accustomed to needing an extractor fan in the kitchen. And what do extractor fans do? They suck out the air; it's their job – air that is keeping the stove alight. Even tumble dryers can have fans built in that interfere with the flue gases. It is essential that your installer carries out a spillage test on the appliance to ensure that it operates safely.

For this very reason many open-flued appliances, like Agas, should not be located in the same room as extractor fans, and manufacturers are at great pains to tell you so. The regulations have for a while drawn attention to this problem and have sometimes advised that fans with greatly reduced extract rates may be acceptable, but it is best not to try and combine the two at all.

If you are installing an open-flued boiler, stick it in the garage or somewhere that has plenty of air flow and doesn't need extractor fans. I do appreciate that sticking the wife out there to cook the Christmas dinner may seem to be a little bit unfair, so with the new stove installed in the kitchen, give the extractor fan a miss or buy the electric-fuelled range. The effects of condensation are not fatal; the effects of carbon monoxide are.

CHAPTER SEVEN

Re-insulating and Ventilating

Replacing or upgrading the thermal insulation in our homes is an almost inevitable task for us all at some point. The older the insulation in the home, the more pressing it becomes, but even properties built 10 or 20 years ago have fallen way behind in what we look for today in thermal insulation standards. The government has driven the standards along in a vehicle known as the Building Regulations, by increasing the energy-efficiency requirements dramatically in recent years. As far as vehicles go, the Building Regulations has behaved more like a shopping trolley lately, by veering off in unexpected directions, but at least in this respect it goes straight up. The standards relate not just to new homes but extensions and alterations in them, and they soon become established as the norm for renovation work as well. Their reason for wanting you to insulate your home is to reduce the nation's CO_2 emissions, a task to which they are committed. Your reason is to reduce your fuel bill and possibly, if there is time, to save the planet later.

 5 Expert Points

HERE ARE FIVE POINTS TO BEAR IN MIND WITH ANY LOFT INSULATION

1 Make sure you insulate in two layers, the first between the ceiling joists and the second, running across the joists (in the other direction) over the top.

2 Insulate the back of the loft trap hatch door.

3 Lag water pipes with an approved phenolic foam lagging, and make sure it fits snugly together with the joints taped.

4 Check that any vapour barriers installed are on the warm (room) side of the insulation and not the cold side.

5 The loft space will be much colder afterwards, so check to see if adequate ventilation exists to keep condensation away. Extra air vents may have to be installed. Tiles vents, eaves vents and gable wall vents are available for remedial installation to improve the cross-flow of air.

Wear protective clothing and a mask for laying insulation.

Friendly insulation

Insulation products might be friendly to the planet, but they aren't all friendly to us. The sad truth is that for too long we've been using unhealthy materials because they've been available, popular and relatively cheap. The fact that you're advised to wear a mask, gloves and even goggles when handling the stuff tells you that it isn't good for your health. The fibres break away when you handle it, becoming airborne for some time, until either they settle or you inhale them. They irritate the skin, causing rashes at a touch, and once in place they collect dust and debris so that one day when somebody comes to replace it they can add a few decades of efficiently collected dirt and dust to the list of horrors. In some ways it's hard to imagine a more unfriendly material. To avoid all that you can buy it wrapped in a protective polythene bag, but you still have to cut this material to fit it, and that's when it turns on you: the fibrous ends produce even finer airborne particles than glass and mineral-fibre quilts, and the exposed edges are sharp and capable of cutting your skin as well as irritating it.

There are some alternatives that

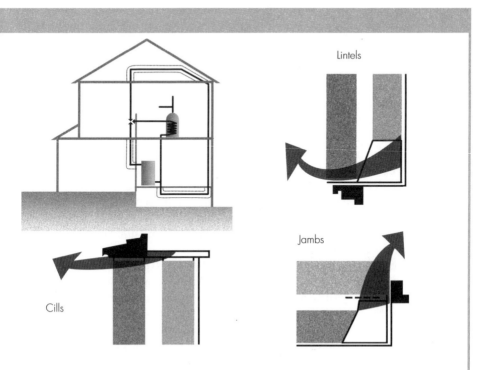

Lintels

Jambs

Cills

Lag pipes and insulate lintels and around window peripheries and cills to combat cold-bridging.

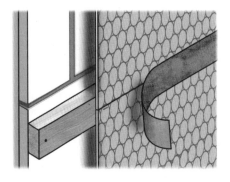

Laminated aluminium sheet insulation with taped joints.

seem a lot more friendly: laminated multi-layer materials enclosed in aluminium foil that don't harbour dust or release particles when cut. Cutting can be done cleanly by scissors without waste, and the joints are sealed together with aluminium tape. Not only that, but they are able to achieve the same insulation levels in a 25 mm thick multi-laminate layer as glass-fibre quilt in a 200 mm thick one. Being new they are more expensive, but as they become more widely used, the price should come down.

It is a fact that if you needed to comply with the Building Regulations for loft insulation with just glass fibre laid between the ceiling joists, it would need to be knee-deep. In practice, two layers are used to reduce overall depth with one laid over the joists and the other between them, but the thickness still prevents you boarding out the loft for access and getting around up there.

Not surprisingly, many builders find it difficult to keep up with the ever-increasing standards for insulation.

They prefer to find a product that's easily available and in dimensions that work, and stick with it on all of their jobs. It takes them time to get to grips with an acceptable specification when the standards change. For the manufacturers of insulation life couldn't be better: they can take advantage of this confusion by creating standard specifications using their products alone and marketing them convincingly to builders as the only way to comply with the regulations.

Because insulation producers tend to specialise in one particular material and not several, they promote its use exclusively. The ability to combine two different materials to achieve a more cost-effective and efficient solution is seldom explored. Take the combination of the aluminium foil-coated bubble-wrap products, which by themselves may only get you halfway to a compliant insulation of walls and roofs, and any other insulation material, and the results can be impressive and economic. Combining products means you can go back to using thinner, more manageable thicknesses of glass fibre, which can mean being able to walk around in the loft again or being able to use 50 x 100 mm timber studs in walls.

Sound insulation

You may be thinking 'Why should I include sound insulation in my renovation work? It's a house, not a recording studio', and you have a point. Our standards for what is acceptable sound insulation between homes were only upgraded in 2003. We just hadn't bothered to do anything worthwhile in the house building industry to reduce noise in our homes before then. Even if you are renovating a detached home with no party walls or floors to worry about, you can take some easy steps to reduce noise between rooms.

The 2003 requirement for internal structures is a minimum of 40 decibels in airborne sound resistance, which is a fairly easy amount to achieve using standard upgrading methods in floors and walls. Decibels are not easy things to visualise, so if it helps to imagine how much sound that is they represent, consider that the rustle of leaves in an autumn breeze can generate 10 decibels, whispering may be 20, and soft music from a radio 40. Normal conversation should generate about 60 decibels and busy traffic 80 – not the other way around, as I often tell my family. If you have to yell to make yourself heard at 2 m, the background noise is around 85 decibels, and this is the kind of noise we look for in fire alarms to wake us up. Above, at the top end of the harmful range, is the painful scream of a jet aircraft at 140. So basically we have an internal sound insulation standard that should just about cut out the soft music of a radio, but not a lively conversation. You might want to improve on that.

Noise does seem to bother us – complaints made to Environmental Health Departments about noisy neighbours, traffic and industry trebled between 1986 and 1996, and they now log over 5,000 per million head of population. Homes built before 2004 have been poorly constructed from a sound-insulation viewpoint, as the standards that applied until then had been kicking around since the 1950s and were not particularly onerous. Not only that, but due to site workmanship and bad design, the Building Research Establishment estimated that about 40 per cent of party walls built didn't meet the standard anyway, and about 25 per cent of floors separating dwellings (like flats and maisonettes) didn't either.

I don't think people have got noisier in recent years, but certainly our entertainment has: TVs and music systems have advanced cinema-like sound with a lot of low-frequency in it, and now when sound insulation is measured it has to be against a reading that includes this low-frequency noise. That, and the fact that more of us are working from home and are stressed out from over-working at that, may have made us more susceptible. Either way, we all value a little peace and quiet, and you can build that in when you renovate.

Floors have become worse in recent times because of the fashion for hard surfaces instead of carpet. Bare boards, laminates and tiles are great to keep clean, but are not good for sound insulation. When you are laying floor finishes, you can achieve a lot by sandwiching a soft isolating material between them and the floor somewhere. With the original boards up and the joists exposed, some sound-lagging materials are designed to be stapled to the joist tops before the boarding is fixed back down. They are made of wool or foam bonded to short strips of MDF, so the boards can then be laid down without any fixing to the joists, thus isolating them from the transmission of impact sound, such as footsteps from above. Other products can overlay the boarding and provide separation in the same way to any floor covering laid above. It's important that that floor covering is floated and not fixed through for these methods to work, and of course you need to be able to raise the floor finish a little. Phenolic foam sheeting, however, is only a few millimetres thick.

Floors don't just suffer with impact sound: airborne sound from rooms above or below works its way through, and only by adding some mass in the construction can it be effectively reduced. This used to be done by using sand pugging between the joists, but that's a bit antiquated now and even bagged, the sand gets everywhere. Mineral-fibre insulation can be used, but you need the heavy stuff, not that used for thermal insulation but the higher-density material designed for sound, and certainly nothing less than 10 kg per cubic metre. Much higher densities are available.

Because you are trying to beef up the weight of the floor here, using extra plasterboard will also help. This is the opposite approach to the resilient layer on top of the floor for impact sound, which actually will work better the lower the density. In this position you are aiming for softness. If they are too thick, resilient layers can add an unwelcome sponginess to your floating floor that could leave you and your furniture feeling a little seasick. You may be able to overcome this by supporting the edges of your floorboarding on battens fixed around the perimeter wall of a room, but you need to turn the resilient layer up behind the batten first to isolate it from the wall. Any floorboarding needs some room for movement and expansion, so you should leave it back a bit from the walls and the skirting and up a bit from the boards; you can fill a 5 mm gap with silicone mastic to seal it but keep it flexible.

Walls can be upgraded, but how much depends on how much room space you can afford to lose. If you're plasterboarding a studwork wall, having taken off the old plaster you can incorporate some mineral-fibre quilt between the studs; again the high density stuff is better, or you can include a plywood or OSB (oriented strand board) sheet first and plasterboard over the top. A doubled-up layer of plasterboard will also increase the fire resistance as well as the sound. Staggering the joints of the boards is important.

Working on masonry walls is much harder: all you can really do to make a difference is to form an independent inner leaf by plasterboarding over a separated studwork frame. The frame has to be set back from the wall by 10 mm or so to ensure that there is a clear cavity behind it, before a sound insulating quilt can be dressed between the studs and the plasterboarding carried out. You can buy acoustic mastic sealant to point around the edges and seal it up from any air passages that noise might leak through.

Cavity-wall insulation

Remedial cavity-wall insulation has been around almost as long as double-glazing, and in the 1980s it was all the rage. For the moment it seems that the canvassing has gone out of it, but there was a time when you could scarcely open your front door without a rep thrusting a leaflet in your hand; now

Installing blown cavity-wall insulation.

reps seem resigned to hovering in the foyers of DIY stores. The benefits of cavity-wall insulation haven't changed, however nor have the potential side effects, and in terms of cost it has been very economical.

For £200 or £300 today most of us with suitable cavity-walled homes can have some mineral fibre pumped into them in two or three hours. In the 80 sq m of the average home's wall,

you could save 80 tonnes of carbon dioxide being released into the atmosphere and about 35 per cent of the heat from your home. The government would like us all to have it done and collectively reduce carbon emissions by almost 40 million tonnes in doing so, but there are drawbacks.

For much of the 20th century we built our homes with clear cavities in the belief that the cavity was a rain barrier that would keep our homes dry. In the 1980s we started building with the cavities filled with insulation and haven't looked back since. As our regulations have demanded more and more thermal insulation, all that's changed is the thickness of the cavity and the insulation we fill it with.

Warranties were needed after injected walls became damp from wind-driven rain. The previously clear cavity had been doing a good job, but with it filled, damp had found a path across to the inside. If you've lived in your home for a few winters you probably know which walls are exposed to the worst weather. Typically, southwest and northeast walls get the worst, but of course this varies from house to house and how sheltered each elevation is; a strategically placed tree or a neighbouring building can make all the difference to shelter, so exposure can vary a lot. Rendered walls or walls clad with timber or tiles are usually well protected if they are in sound condition, but face brickwork is always vulnerable. You can tell when it's wet, not least of all because the shade darkens and can stay that way for

143

prolonged wet periods – and therein lies the problem: if insulation does get wet it stays wet, and only by opening up the cavity and removing it can you solve the problem.

In April 1995 the Cavity Insulation Guarantee Agency (CIGA) was launched to provide an installer's warranty for the work that would cover the home-owner for failures. For a one-off payment you can buy insurance for a period of 25 years, which should see you through a few wet winters – even with global warming in the offing.

Because of increasing standards you might not be able to achieve the same levels of thermal insulation that a new home would have, but it could still make a huge difference. When cavity fill first became available, different products were around from polystyrene beads to urea formaldehyde foam and glass fibres; like Betamax videos, most became extinct, leaving mineral fibre as the preferred material. Pumped in through holes in the brickwork, the mineral fibres expand to fill the cavity as best they can and hold in some of that valuable heat. The holes that they drill in your brickwork aren't big but they aren't quite small enough either. Aimed at the corners of mortar joints they can take off the corners of some bricks, leaving a tell-tale sign that the job has been done after the mortar repair has gone off. It is subtle, but once you see it, you can recognise it straight away. If you are replastering your home inside or rendering outside, you have the advantage of being able

to inject the cavities first from in or out and cover the holes for good.

Before installers inject your walls, they are supposed to inspect them and determine their suitability. If the wall construction doesn't suit it or if the cavities are blocked or contain electrical cables, problems can occur. In the case of the latter, electrical cables shouldn't be in the cavity of the wall, but if they are and they become encased in insulation, they could overheat and start a fire.

In some homes cavities have been ventilated with air bricks, a practice that has since stopped, but if you have vents serving indoor spaces they should be sleeved through the wall cavity itself.

Remedial cavity-wall insulation has been a self-regulating industry where the installers have to submit notices to the local authority. These notices describe the materials and BBA accreditation and the accreditation of the installer as well as the address and date of the work. They don't attract Building Control fees or general inspections, and really amount to self-certification statements.

Advantages
- Saves up to 70 per cent of heat loss

- Not disruptive

- Doesn't add anything to the wall thickness

- Relatively cheap

- Quick to have installed (2–3 hours)

Disadvantages

- May cause damp in exposed brick walls

- Cavity must be in a reasonable condition

- Minor damage to brickwork in drilling and filling holes

- Requires a particular cavity wall construction of masonry (not timber or metal frame) with a clear cavity (typically 50–75 mm wide)

- Foam-type insulation and adhesive bonded ones give off gases

Points to check with the work

- Make sure that the cavities have been inspected first

- Check that the top of cavities are sealed

- Check that any air bricks, vents or flues are sleeved

- Check that no electrical wiring exists without being de-rated inside cavities

- Make sure your installer and insulation are BBA registered and CIGA registered

Solid-wall insulation

Internal lining

Without the luxury of a cavity in your external walls, you are faced with only two options for improving the insulation: inside or out. Out is only an option if you plan to change the appearance of the walls with a rendered or clad finish, so it may be no choice at all. Inside will of course reduce the room sizes, but perhaps not by as much as you'd think.

Foil-based multi-laminates lend themselves to wall-renovation work. They come in rolls of 25 m or more, and can be safely handled. To treat walls you have to suspend and pin them to timber battens, so that they hang in a narrow void behind the boarded finish, but even so the total thickness is not great. The joints are sealed together with aluminium tape to create a warm envelope for the room that can reduce the heat loss through a solid old brick wall to a quarter of its former self.

The higher the performance of the material, the higher the cost, but some are not as expensive as you might think and can still do an excellent job. Look for the thermal resistance of these products in the manufacturer's data and compare them with other materials like glass fibre and polystyrene, and you will see that multi-laminates outperform them by huge amounts.

In the past, plasterboard materials pre-bonded to polyurethane foam sheets were used for dry-lining solid walls, and these remain available but scarce in domestic use. The cost has probably driven away many potential users, together with the fact that you need a considerable thickness to achieve something worth doing. There is also the problem of creating a soft inner wall that is very difficult to fix

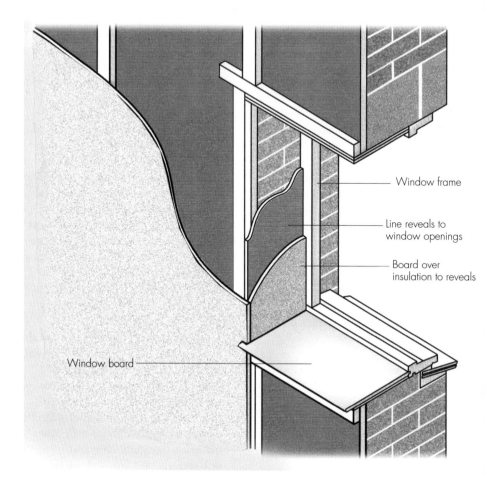

Window frame

Line reveals to window openings

Board over insulation to reveals

Window board

Internal insulation with dry-lined finish.

anything to without a cavity behind the boarding to open a plug into.

Advantages
- Ideal in older homes with solid walls

- Ideal for treating individual rooms

- Ideal for heating rooms quickly

- Ideal for reducing condensation by creating a warm, dry surface in a heated room

Disadvantages
- Skirtings, covings, rails, electric switches and sockets and radiators all need to be refixed

- Room size is slightly reduced

● Disruption to your living space

Points to check with the work
● Face of wall should be well-sealed

● A vapour barrier (eg polythene) is essential behind the plasterboard

● Insulation needs to be sealed with approved tape around all the service entries and joints

● Make sure insulation lining and plasterboarding is turned into the reveals and soffits of window and door openings

External lining
If your renovation work includes re-cladding parts of your home outside, then you could explore the possibility of insulating behind the cladding. Even rendered walls can incorporate insulation sheeting in this position, but it is better suited to tile-hung and boarded walls.

Advantages
● Overcomes thermal bridging through variations in the wall

● Reduces room temperature variations

● Internal services, wall fixtures and decor aren't affected

● Less disruption to your living space

Disadvantages
● External cladding needs to be replaced

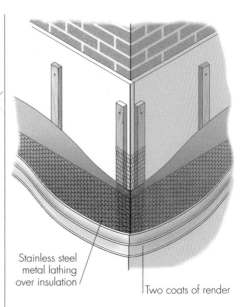

Stainless steel metal lathing over insulation

Two coats of render

External insulating and render finish.

● Wall thickness is increased

● Rainwater goods and plumbing wastes need to be refixed.

● Expensive

Points to check with the work
● Lining and cladding must extend into the window and door reveals

● Cladding often needs a ventilated cavity between it and the insulation

● Rendering can only be done in mild, dry weather

● Light-coloured rendering finish helps to reflect heat in summer

147

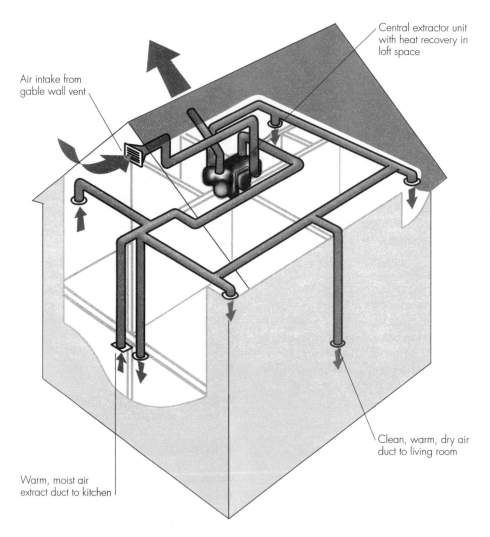

Central extractor unit with heat recovery in loft space

Air intake from gable wall vent

Clean, warm, dry air duct to living room

Warm, moist air extract duct to kitchen

The ductwork extracts stale air and distributes clean air to rooms.

Whole-house ventilation

Not everybody has or wants the ability to leave windows open when they're at home. For one thing, there is the security angle and the risk of

forgetting not to close and lock them when you nip off to the shops, and then there is the noise and pollution of urban life, like living near a busy road or airport. Becoming increasingly popular are whole-house ventilation systems that provide every room with circulating air, whether they have windows open or not. The noisy and ugly extractor fans that occupy kitchens and bathrooms can also be dispensed with if you have a low-power central extracting system. These can be fitted remedially to homes, but it helps if your renovation work is extensive enough to form duct passages through walls and floors.

You need either a cupboard or a loft space in which to house an extractor fan, but these fans can be fairly compact now. The loft is an ideal place to house these units, although they are relatively quiet running and could be located in a top floor cupboard. Used to draw up the damp air from the house via ductwork, they resemble a box-like octopus with arms of flexible ductwork extending out at all angles into the home, and a built-in heat-recovery capacity separates the warm air and re-employs it to heat fresh new air coming in.

Fresh air can also be cooled down by heat exchangers as well as heated up by them and in the summer months this process also helps to de-humidify the air coming in: not air-conditioning (although that can't be far away in Britain if we get more summers like 2003), but a more energy-efficient version of it. Levels of heat recovery for different units vary from 65 to 95 per cent, so almost none of the heat used to warm your home is wasted by extraction, something which conventional extractor fans are very good at. If you've ever stood outside by an extractor fan outlet on a really cold day and felt the heat being pushed out, you'll understand the benefits of heat-recovery extraction immediately.

If there is any maintenance to be done, apart from servicing the motor occasionally, it will involve redecorating around the extract points where the removal of dirty air can cause pattern staining on the ceiling. Your ability to install a system like this will depend a lot on how much work you can do to build the ductwork into the home and, most importantly in houses, into the walls. In bungalows such a system will be no problem to use with ceiling grills only.

Given the loss of noisy fans, the house becomes a lot more comfortable sound-wise. Comfort also gets improved by continuous 24-hour circulation of fresh air day and night, and with filters on the air entry points, the air coming in can be cleaned of pollen and pollutants. I've seen these systems used in new self-built homes where the owners have suffered from hay fever or asthma, but I'm told they are also good for removing tobacco smoke or animal smells from the home before furnishings and finishings become impregnated with them. Respiratory illness is on the up, and near on one in five children experience asthmatic symptoms, so cleaning the air in our homes seems like a good idea.

CHAPTER EIGHT

Redecorating

Reflooring

Carpet

In 2003, TV ads with the message 'Come back to carpet' were launched with an attractive young lady rolling around on a nice shagpile. Clearly the carpet industry had stopped and they were trying to resuscitate it, presumably by suggesting that there were some things you could do on a carpeted floor that you couldn't do on a hard-finished floor – at least that's how I read it.

I think it may have been too late, or perhaps too early, because the overriding perception of carpet at this time was of a nesting site for dust mites and fleas, to say nothing of the mass of human dead skin that has to be continually vacuumed out. Hygiene is not one of carpet's attributes, and this fact has been driven home by laminate floors since the mid-1990s.

It'll be back, I'm sure, and in some rooms there just seems to be no beating it – bedrooms, for example. Stepping out of bed onto a hard-boarded floor first thing on a winter's morning just doesn't hold the same attraction. But as well as comfort and warmth, carpet holds one other benefit; it absorbs sound very efficiently. Impact sound is considerably reduced by a quality underlay, and so many times in the past has this fact been given to me by developers trying to avoid sound-insulating flats. They had a point, of course, but carpet can be easily lifted and exchanged for laminate or

whatever else comes along as the vogue of the day. It's a furnishing and not part of the construction.

In renovating a period family home, carpet has some benefit, though – it's forgiving and doesn't care much if the floor is off-level or uneven.

Preparing the floor

If you are planning on replacing carpet with laminate or tiles, you may have some repairs to do first. Ground floors need to be reasonably level if they are to take hard finishings. Kitchen floors can't be anything but level beneath the cupboards; some cupboard units have levelling feet that can be adjusted, but compared to a level floor they are a nightmare to align in rows for a continuous worktop.

If your floors are solid but simply old and a bit higgledy-piggeldy, levelling compound can be used to finish them. This is a self-levelling product that finishes to a cementatious surface, smooth and bump-free, after being simply poured on – no trowelling or any other mucking about. You might have to prime the existing floor first after cleaning it, and some professionals like to use a decorator's roller on the finish to get any bubbles out that might appear just before it cures.

If the floor is seriously out of level and self-levelling compound can't be used, you should consider screeding it. Conventional sand and cement mixes are fine down to about 50 mm thick, but beneath that they have a tendency to crack up. If the floor needs to be repaired in certain areas but is fine in others, your answer lies with epoxy-resin mortars that are designed to patch up damaged concrete floors. Again, these have depth limits that lie between that of self-levelling and that of screed – up to about 25 mm thick. You don't normally need to prime the existing concrete before using them, but you will need to have an application kit: tools such as a float trowel, wire brush, vinyl gloves – nothing expensive, as the product will be all the expense you'll want.

Timber-boarded floors can easily be repaired, as traditional boards are square-edged and don't interlock. Lifting damaged boards and replacing them can be supplemented by filling any excessive gaps between boards with timber slips. Gaps can appear when movement has caused the floor to creep out of level, and if they aren't filled you may suffer from draughts as well as a nightly invasion of wildlife – I'm thinking slugs here, which seem to be able to squeeze through the tiniest of gaps and find the voids beneath ground floors ideal places to raise a family. All those DIY TV shows show sanded-down floorboards, but this isn't always a good idea; if you go ahead, old paint and lacquer can be stripped off with solvent and the boards can be finished with wax – varnish creates a glossy and yellowy finish that can deteriorate in sunlight, although it does make the floor easier to wipe clean.

Solid wood floors

Traditional tongue-and-grooved floorboards are still available in softwood, but seldom do you see a whole room boarded out with them, if ever. As repairs to an existing floor, new softwood is often pieced in to replace split and rotten boards, but here's the rub: the moisture content of timber and the fact that the wood is cut from the tree with little waste has meant that new timber boards tend to curl up with the grain when they dry out.

I see it all the time: kiln-dried timber that looks fine on the delivery lorry starts to bend as soon as it arrives in the central heating of the British home; and if you have underfloor heating, don't even consider it. In the past, when timber demand was less and our environmental ethics were even scarcer, wood was cut from the heart out to give a straighter grain in cross-section. Now, softwood timber used in construction is more likely to have been cut from the outer edge of the tree, slicing across with the curve of the grain – economical and environmental, but no good for floorboarding.

The curving effect, particularly across the width of the board, is disastrous for furniture and unpleasant to see and walk on. In time boards dry out, but how long I can't say. Suppliers recommend that you stand the timber in the room to acclimatise it first, and this is even true with laminates, but I've known kiln-dried timber be left to stand in an unheated new or renovated home absorbing moisture happily until it is laid and the heating is put on. They do mean a dry, heated room for acclimatisation!

Natural wood floors do have their good points. They are free from solvents and formaldehydes if they are a glueless system, they look wonderful (when flat) and they can be hard-wearing and last for ages. Better-quality ones have their ends treated with hard wax oil made from natural sources, to resist accidents, although if you think you are likely to be spilling a lot of fluids, you should seal the surface of the floor as well with hard wax oil. The wood will still be able to breathe, but this product also affords it some scratch resistance from children and moving chairs (or chairs and moving children).

Because of the noise generated by footfalls on a solid floor, some boarding comes with a bonded damping mat attached to the underside of the board to isolate it a bit from the floor joists. These mats are thin and may not amount to the equivalent sound reduction achieved by carpet, perhaps only as much as 10 decibels. From an environmental point of view, many acoustic underlays are made from recycled materials such as car tyres and other waste products, which is commendable, but armed with the words 'acoustic' or 'sound insulation', they are, in 2003 anyway, priced optimistically. Basic phenolic foam underlay used beneath laminate offers some resistance to impact sound, simply because as a floating layer, it separates the hard surfaces of the floorboarding and the laminate flooring, creating a break in the air path. The problem is that with the hard surface the impact sound is converted to airborne, with echoing reverberation that is much worse.

Because timber improves with age and can easily be restored to its best appearance with a powered sander and some sealer, it is always worth researching and buying secondhand salvaged floor finishings. The wood will have been seasoned and cut before the last decades of the 20th century, making it much more likely to be of a better quality than that available new today. Old public buildings, schools and institutions up for demolition are ideal sources of quality hardwood flooring, as well as salvage yards – if you can't get to it before they do. Some of the best floors I've seen have been salvaged from school gymnasiums and army barracks demolished after 50 years' service or more. You will need to spend some time sanding down and sealing the surface, but with wood the more effort you put into preparing it, the more it rewards you with its warmth and beauty.

Laminate flooring

About the same time that the recessed halogen light fad took off in the late 1990s, the laminate floor market rose; and at that time it was 'wood-effect' laminates with a hard-wearing melamine finish veneered to MDF that proved popular and cheap. Laminates were a fraction of the price of carpet, and the average-sized room could be done for £100. Laminates are a good choice for that reason alone, but also, because they require no surface treatment, they are the lino of the Millennium. Like any fad they will undoubtedly become loathed because

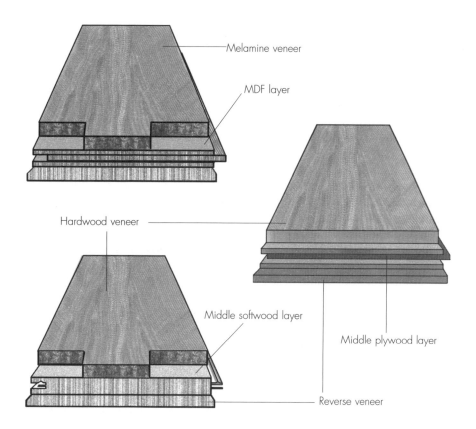

Melamine veneer

MDF layer

Hardwood veneer

Middle softwood layer

Middle plywood layer

Reverse veneer

The choice of laminate flooring.

of their popularity, but you can't escape from the fact that at least one room in every family home would benefit from having a cheap laminate floor that can be played on by children, walked on by pets and just wiped clean at the end of the day. With the appearance of wood and the cleanliness of tiles, laminates will always be incredibly functional.

Because laminates are made up in layers, better-quality ones use natural wood veneers instead of a melamine surface. With the layers bonded together and the natural timber only about 4 mm thick, the effects of drying out are less harsh than with solid timber boarding, and they can normally be laid to a flat surface and expected to stay that way.

Some boards that have a natural-wood veneer on both faces and plywood sandwiched between them will need an extended period of acclimatisation, although typically the underside is of thinner and cheaper softwood, such as spruce, and the topside is hardwood. These better-quality laminate floors tend to be around 15 mm thick.

With any type of laminate the boards are either glued or snap-locked together. With the former, they are usually glued at the edges and cranked into each other with a ratchet cramp until dry, so the important part of laying them is to keep an expansion gap around the perimeter. Strips of cork or some other compressible material will achieve this, but they do need to be rigid and uniform enough to command a straight edge.

With any boarded floor it is absolutely essential that you start square against the wall before heading into the room; a fraction out here will become a crevasse when you get to the other side. Laminate flooring is particularly unforgiving in this respect; because it is machine-made to fine tolerances, it tends to show up out-of-square rooms. Do not be tempted to lay it up to the existing skirting boards and use an odd piece of fillet or beading to join the two together unless you have some exceptional reason.

Skirting board is easy to remove and replace; you just need to think of it as part of the floor finish and not the wall. You could take the opportunity to upgrade the skirting to something more attractive with a deeper section or ogee moulding that will frame the floor nicely. When you replace skirting it covers the edge of the floor and will cope with some small indifference, but at best it tends only to be 25 mm thick, so clearly there are limits.

Cork

Cork is a species of oak that is different from any other. It is soft and has unique attributes that other woods don't possess. Popular in wall tiling in the 1970s, it has been out of fashion ever since, but it could make a comeback in flooring because it is soft and warm and quiet – everything that carpet is – without the bugs. Apart from a sheep's-wool rug, it is the only natural product you can lay on a floor that has inherent sound insulation against footfalls. Environmentally, cork is a good choice as it can be harvested without felling the tree, and only once it has reached maturity. Things grow slowly in the Mediterranean, and cork trees don't reach maturity until they are 30 years of age. They give up the bark easily, and a decade later it has regrown, ready to be stripped again in what is a traditional manual industry of Spain and Portugal.

Cork flooring is now produced like tongue-and-groove jointed laminate, about 10 to 12 mm thick for glueless joints in pieces around 1 m long. It is ideal for bedrooms where carpet isn't wanted and the noise and hardness of wood aren't either. Nor does it shrink or suffer from the moisture-absorbing problems of other woods. Children's bedrooms are ideal for cork flooring, giving them enough of a cushion to break a fall and still be clean and hygienic. Cork can also be sealed with hard wax oil, or can even be varnished for extra protection. Use oils that are derived from natural plant extracts and are suitable for allergy sufferers and asthmatics.

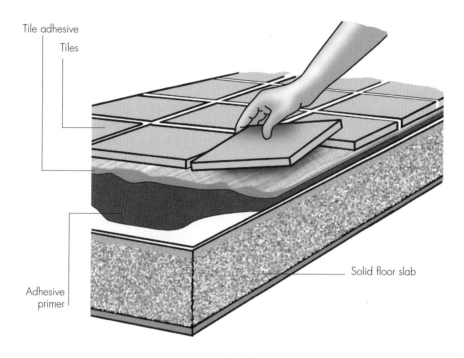

Tile adhesive

Tiles

Adhesive
primer

Solid floor slab

Laying a tiled floor.

However, cork does have its downsides. For one thing, you pretty much have to like the colour beige, and for another, it isn't cheap. And if you're not careful, the whole floor can look like a notice pinboard.

Tiles and slabs

Up recently, floor tiling was pretty much restricted to the kitchens of British homes, but since then, thanks to the improved tile adhesives, tiles have been taken to bathrooms and hallways. For these hard-working areas that need hard surfacing and surfacing

that doesn't mind getting wet occasionally, tiles are the quality choice, and the vast range of materials and design continues to expand the available choice.

In kitchens, traditional quarry tiles give that farmhouse look, and they have always worked well in Victorian or Edwardian houses. Ceramics tend to be imported from Spain and Portugal and vary a good deal in quality and price, but they can be relatively cheap; and designer Italian tiles can be, like everything else Italian, pointlessly expensive. The real problem with tiles is the fact that in Britain we have always had to pay twice as much as the rest of Europe for them. Forget booze cruising: if you can nip over the Channel to fill your car with tiles from a French DIY store, it is worth the trip. The same tiles are available as over here, but at greatly reduced prices – a tile specialist shop in Britain is an expensive place to visit, and I'm at loss to understand why.

The tile choice doesn't stop at ceramics, of course, which can be a little slippery when wet, but extends into the natural stone range. Granite, limestone and slate each have distinctive features and look superb in any home, regardless of its age.

Perhaps more than anything, the size of tiles needs to be correctly proportioned to the size of the floor. Large tiles in a small room like a bathroom can give the floor a patio look, and make it seem smaller. Too small and it becomes a jigsaw puzzle, so finding the right size of tile is as important as finding the right colour and pattern.

Stone flooring has been reserved for external use, such as in patios, until the recent trend for using natural products indoors, but you don't have to bed them in cement and sand mortar as if they were in the garden. Manufacturers have caught up, and pourable bedding mixes are available that are thick enough to make up for all the imperfections and uneven surfaces present on the back of stone tiles. These pre-mixes simply need an amount of water added and a trowelled application to get them

down. You could think of them as halfway between a tile adhesive and a floor screed. Stone slab floors are best laid with dry kiln-dried sand brushed between the joints; don't be tempted to point them with cement joints or seal them with wax or oil.

Floors and heating

Conventional heating, beyond running hot water pipes through holes in the joists, will have no direct effect on a timber or laminate floor. Heating a renovated room is going to dry it out suddenly, and some movement is inevitable.

Underfloor heating is perfect for tiled floors, but is not such a good idea for timber floors; the idea of heating your new floor finish to effectively convert it into a radiator should be enough to tell you that. With underfloor heating, your floor is your radiator. Some systems, notably electric ones, do say that they can be used with any floor structure or finish, but are they going to replace it when it bows out of shape?

There are also heating skirting systems around that utilise either water-filled copper pipework concealed in purpose-made plastic skirting or electric heating cables concealed in purpose-made plastic channels. Given standard skirting board sizes, I can't imagine the rated output is going to be enough to heat a room unless it is left on permanently, but they are out there, and if all you want is a low level of background warmth, they could be what you're looking for.

Redecorating

If you're renovating to sell your home, it is usually wise to keep your personal taste for colour and décor locked in a cupboard. Using whites, creams and beige colours on the walls and floors may seem bland, but they give a fresh and clean look to the home, and that is always acceptable. People tend to be able to visualise their own ideas for décor better over a blank canvas than over the top of somebody else's creativity.

For you, however, the rules are there to be broken, and some of us really like to break them: mixing several styles to create décor chaos, or choosing colours that clash, and not being able to settle for one feature wall and making three, or using conflicting patterns.

Feature walls are simply those that are different to the other walls in a room, the one out of the four in any room that draws the eye and takes away from the feeling that you have just walked into a shoebox. You may be lucky enough to have a room with a feature wall built-in, as it were, to your home's construction. It might be built from a different material, like stone, or have an exposed timber framework, or may just frame an architectural feature like a fireplace or an arched window. Most of us, however, have to create a feature wall with décor. The easiest way to achieve this is with colour. Finding a complementary colour, one that is different enough but still in harmony with the rest of the room, is the challenge. A colour wheel will save you from making a terrible mistake at this point; because feature walls need to catch the eye but not offend it, they must be in balance with the other colours in the room, and not all colours work with each other.

If you thought you might dip out by having a subtle difference in shade, the wall isn't going to make it as a feature: it needs to be obvious. Some of the immediacy about the colour change here may be reduced when the room is furnished and creatively lit, so give it a chance to settle in before you reach for the trade-size can of matt white.

If you can't bring yourself to use an accent colour to pick out a wall, think about texture and what coverings you could use beyond smooth plaster and emulsion. Paint effects take time to apply well, but they can look dramatic when applied to a single wall. A sand-finished texture or a metallised finish is all that's needed to add interest. Where textures don't work so well is everywhere at once – paint effects have a place in my world, but it's a small one.

Patterns can also work, whether they be bold stripes of colour or a transitional shading of colour to white. You start with a base colour at floor level and gradually work up the wall in bands, mixing the paint with a tad more white to each band. The trick is to use a dry, soft brush to smudge out the joints between bands and blend them together to create an imperceptible change in colour throughout the height of the wall. It takes time and patience to get it right, but it is worth it. Start with the full colour at ceiling level and work towards a white skirting, if you like – whatever flies your kite.

The illusion of space

With modern homes becoming smaller in size, the task of creating the illusion of space falls on the decorating and furnishing.

If you're thinking that you'll have to adopt the show-home trick of leaving all the internal doors off and building smaller purpose-made beds, think again. Some things that you can live with work well, such as glass-topped tables, glass-walled cabinets and furniture with slender legs, all of which allow you to see the full floor area of the room. Things that will work against you to steal the floor area, like chairs and settees on castors, floor base kitchen units and dark floor coverings, are to be avoided. Lighting beneath cabinets to pick out the floor finish, and placing mirrors in strategic areas will also help enormously.

Many developers now see the space beneath the stairs, which for years we all knew as the broom cupboard, as a study. How can anybody study beneath a staircase, deprived or light, headroom and privacy? Not even Harry Potter can work beneath a staircase, and if it's an open-plan stair, that's all the more reason to leave it that way, as any attempt to 'develop' it will look cluttered and ill-conceived. If you need to use the space for something, build in a purpose-made cabinet that has been made to measure with large doors and small drawers. A MDF cabinet front could be painted in with the room or maybe even become the feature wall.

Reflecting the light around, white shades and colours such as yellow and pale blue are space-creators, while deep colours like reds and dark blues absorb light and eat space – fine if your Goth teenager wants to live in a bat cave, but not so fine for making your living room appear spacious.

Renovating period décor

Homes go through periods in their life and don't tend to stick to one: original features are taken out and replaced, décor gets updated, and a 'period home' may have lost the period of its origin along the way. If you are planning on renovating it back to its original self, you might want to consider just how authentic you want the decorating to be.

I know that for some, who have gone to the trouble of renovating to the original architecture and restoring (or replacing) the original features, going the whole nine yards and decorating it in the period style will be just as important. But the downside is that this will ultimately mean using colours that were available and traditional at that time, and that will place some limitations upon you that you can't live with. How far you decide to go down the path of authenticity is up to you – for most of us, it's as far as it suits us.

From a research point of view, the services of an interior design architect and the RIBA are invaluable. Said to be the world's largest collection of its kind, the RIBA holds a library of over 600,000 design drawings for buildings and their interiors, reaching back to the 15th century: detailed drawings of not only buildings, but fabrics, furnishings, ceramics and interiors – in short, everything you need to research a particular style or era for all types of renovation work.

Period colours

In bygone times, when colour pigments were derived from minerals and natural sources, the cost of extracting a pigment from its origins was reflected in the cost of the paint – and the cost of the paint was reflected in where it was used. Earthy colours made from lime wash and tinted with clay represented the cheapest colours in the palette, and these were used to paint kitchens, corridors and servants' quarters. Green, derived from copper, was much more expensive and was therefore used only in important rooms where the owners wished to receive guests and have them recognise their wealth and status. If you plan to truly renovate your period home to its original authentic decor, you should also respect the hierarchy of colour.

The paint-making and mixing technology available to us today has nothing to do with localised soil conditions and the availability of minerals and pigments, and more to do with the range of shades that the human eye can detect – around 10,000,000. Some major paint manufacturers have produced a range of historic colours developed from

research into period interior design, and these are about as authentic as you can get; they are divided into eight period palettes.

Pre-1850

GOTHIC REVIVAL

In the 1830s and 1840s, Gothic saw a big revival with the early Victorians, who were clearly taken with the style from the previous century. Colours from this range would make an authentic and popular choice for the renovation of a Victorian home built during this revived era. The Palace of Westminster got the same treatment when it was rebuilt at this time, and if you're looking for inspiration, here would be a good place to start – although you might have to scale things down a bit.

REGENCY

Everybody seems to admire Regency colours. They are bold, sumptuous and rich – just the sort of thing we like today. The architect Alexander Roos was the drive behind this infatuation with bright colour and design, inspired by the archaeology in Egypt and Italy at that time. Homes built between 1800 and 1830, before the Gothic Revival, would have been decorated in this way, but the style works just as well in modern homes, particularly those with high ceilings.

NEO-CLASSICAL

Around the mid-1700s architects began to challenge the previous rigid styles and look towards more flamboyant and decorative interiors with soft but clear colours and ornate finishings. Rooms in this style are tied together to create a flowing style that shouldn't be broken up with a bit of Gothic Revival or Regency thrown in. Notable architects of the time included William Chambers and Robert Adam, who were influenced by Roman archaeology of the time that revealed just how decorated Roman homes were.

PALLADIAN

Dating from the mid-1600s to mid-1700s, Palladianism has been replicated (perhaps by accident) into recent homes. This is Roman architecture raising its head yet again, but this time the key elements are symmetry and proportion and order – the classic rules of architecture. Interior design colours from this era are in truth quite colourless, with greys, creams and whites predominating and with details picked out more by gentle shades than anything else.

The natural materials popular now, like marble and stone floors – indeed, the whole natural material and textures design fad that has had us placing baskets of Aran pebbles on white marble fireplace hearths and may have peaked at the Millennium – reflects the style of Andrea Palladio quite nicely, if not intentionally.

Post-1850

VICTORIAN ECLECTIC

From the 1860s the Victorians had travel on their minds, and they were greatly influenced by the styles they saw in other countries: the styles of Moorish Spain, the Italian Renaissance, Egypt, India and Japan all began to appear. They had discovered that the world was as wonderfully diverse in terms of architecture as it was in nature. Colours that come with this era can therefore be exotic and vibrant, with oranges and blues, turquoise and emerald. Mixing styles isn't always a workable solution, but you can feel justified with a Victorian home to have a have a Moroccan blue en-suite with Moorish tiles in your Italianate bedroom. If the urge takes you.

ARTS AND CRAFTS

By the end of the 19th century, the Victorians felt disposed to reflect the natural world in their design with bright and cheery designs that were simple but artistic. It was a celebration of their craftsmanship skills (you'd be hard-pushed to revive this era today without using a lot of MDF and a stencil kit), and they certainly had plenty to celebrate.

Flower colours such as yellow and lilac prevailed, and the ambience of the whole style is well suited to country cottages. Charles Voysey was one designer at the forefront of the Arts and Crafts movement.

ART DECO

1920s decadence is represented by this style, which comes with the feel of luxury about it even now. I am a fan of Art Deco, but in homes you have to look hard to find a reference to it, and even the picture palaces (now bingo halls) have managed to lose it amongst the modern high-street scene. The style was typified by the work of designer John Alexander, including his original interior decorating work and plaster mouldings.

1950S
The music of the era might still be popular, but the buildings aren't. It's difficult to think of 1950s architecture as anything that you'd want to recreate, but the interiors were unique. Formica and lino, plus the colours that went with this era, seemed to have been fashioned to offend – lime greens together with brick reds – and anything that could be seen from a long distance and would immediately upset elderly people was in.

Colours and the 21st century

It has been said that a nation's mood is reflected by the colours that pass through its fashions – like during cautious times, when economic growth is fragile and we creep out of a depression, we apparently tend to favour pastel colours like pink and pale blue: soft, gentle and not too bright and optimistic. In times of economic growth and prosperity, bright, bold colours like red and orange are fashionable. If the nation suffers a disaster, war or some other catastrophe, neutral colours like cream and brown become popular.

Colour does go with fashion, and if you're going to follow it you'll either have to keep ahead of the news or redecorate quite often. Imagine if in Britain our colour choice was affected by the weather – the paint would scarcely have time to dry before we'd be sanding it off.

In my book there is only one way to choose colour, and that is by yourself, holding a colour wheel. Colour wheels are circular rainbows that tell you what colours go with what and which ones clash violently. It's important to use colour carefully in a house if you aren't to wake up with a headache everyday or sink into depression each time you use the bathroom.

Colours and mood are linked, but it is more a case of them affecting us than us affecting them. Red, for example, is rich and vibrant, but because it is used in nature and the man-made world to warn us of danger, we tend not to paint much of our homes with it – the front door, perhaps, but not the kitchen, which would look like the ketchup bottle had been shaken with the cap off again. So colour has to be used with the function of the room if it is to work: greens and blues allude to reflections of water and are great for bathrooms, hot colours like reds and oranges for bedrooms, and so on.

Lime wash

Lime wash is most probably the only material that has survived over the years, purely because of restoration work. The use of lime wash as a building material ended decades ago and was replaced with cement. Lime is produced in powder form by quarrying limestone and kiln-baking it to around 1000°C – so don't try making your own. It was the Romans' choice of material. They used it not only for mortar but also render and plaster, and it stuck with us until the 20th century, when a gradual decline in its use began and continued to decline to the end of the century. In the last 20 years, I've only seen it used on the odd church being replastered with lime and sand mixed with goat hair, or on an old brick wall.

Now, however, lime's future is on the up, partly because it has some diverse applications for new work and renovations. It has been making a bit of a comeback in interiors (Palladianism at work again), but you may still have to buy it from a specialist supplier who stocks materials for conservation work. Take lime putty and mix it with water, for example, and you have a good lime wash that you can add pigment to for colour on inside walls. Existing lime-rendered walls can only be treated with lime wash if they aren't too heavily built up with coatings, or where they've not been painted with modern paints. Outside, lime doesn't bond at all well to cement render and isn't that durable, so it needs to be redone more often than you would expect to repaint a wall, perhaps once every year or two.

Light

Science tells us that light is colour in the full spectrum. Interior design tells us that colour without the right light is a waste of time. But light changes continuously – it changes naturally with the passing of the day, and it changes artificially with the lamps we use and how we use them. It never stays the same, so when choosing a colour you have to choose it over a period of time.

Paint a large enough square (at least 300 x 300 mm) on a wall to appreciate the depth of the colour and view it at different times of the day. Try different lamps after dark, and you'll be amazed how your perspective of it can change. You might not like the colour under certain lighting conditions, so the use of the room ties in with the light. If you plan on mostly using the room for eating breakfast in, then clearly it doesn't matter what it looks like in the evening if it looks great in the morning sun.

Because in Britain we have a very special quality to our daylight that can only be achieved by filtering sunshine through 500 feet of cloudbase, we need to see colour in our environment and not somebody else's. An orange seen in the Greek islands is not the same colour as one seen in Britain, because temperature-wise the light is nearer to the cool blue end of the spectrum here, and that takes the edge off of our reds and other warm colours, making them lose some of their vibrancy.

In the final analysis, however, it might also be advisable to leave the colour selection to the fairer sex: apparently 8 per cent of men are colour-blind, compared to only 0.5 per cent of women.

Decorating metalwork

This might sound obvious, but metals are cold materials, and warm, moist air condenses on them. I have seen them exposed in bathrooms and kitchens, but I can't help but think they would stream with surface condensation. Bathrooms tend also to be small spaces where people are sometimes on the verge of wakefulness; and somehow I don't see an eye-level iron flange joining two iron columns together as the ideal thing to meet when you walk in, yet I meet architects who think it is.

Iron structures

Exposing and decorating key metal structures in older buildings is quite fashionable at the moment; they come under the heading of 'original features' that estate agents get excited over. But really they are the bones, the structural elements of the home, and by definition in years to come people will sit beneath the bare-wood trussed rafters of a 1985 home drooling over their original featureness and wondering why they had been plasterboarded over.

Before the 19th century metalwork in buildings was limited to the occasional strap and bolt, but with the industrial age of the mid-19th century came iron. Wrought iron was replaced with cast iron, but wrought iron made a comeback tour between 1850 and 1890 because of its versatility, improved quality and because it could be crafted into so many stylish things; with liberal riveting it could even be made into RSJs. Wrought iron seems to

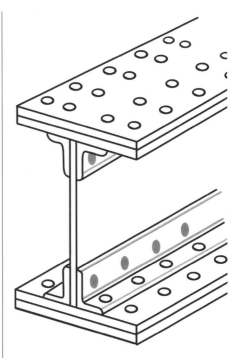

Wrought-iron beam.

have passed the test of time because of its smelting process – instead of coke and coal over charcoal, which coated it with a black magnetic oxide coat, good at inhibiting rust.

We didn't use metal in buildings to any structural end before the turn of the 19th century, when cast-iron frameworks were introduced to industrial design. Later it was discovered that when wrought iron was heated up it could be rolled and shaped to make beams, and that was a big advantage. It had a sort of fibrous and less brittle structure to it than the crystalline form of cast iron, and if you have cast-iron pillars in your home, you might see the mould lines in

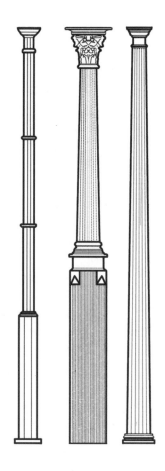

Decorative iron columns.

necessary to clean cast iron before decorating, but in the case of wrought iron, flame-cleaning is possible with a great deal of care.

If any metal structures are features, cast-iron ones are, being usually hollow and circular with end plates and ornate decorations. In beams the bottom flange is often bigger than the top, revealing their identity, but you can also spot them by looking for the signs of surface

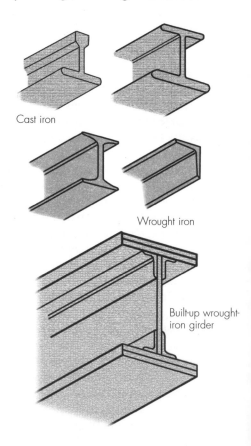

Cast iron

Wrought iron

Built-up wrought-iron girder

them, which tend to fracture with age. Wrought and cast iron are repairable by 'cold–stitching', using a metal-rich epoxy resin, but if the element is structural it may need to be replaced.

Cast-iron features are best suited as non-load-bearing features where any uncertainty exists over their condition or loading. Sandblasting is usually

Variations in ironwork.

cracking that occurred during the cooling process of manufacture.

Wrought-iron beams tend to have more rounded corners and edges, and are regular in shape. Their elasticity meant that they were able to allow some movement without cracking and were likely to be around much longer. Big wrought-iron beams tended to be made up in sections and riveted together.

If your home has been converted from a Victorian industrial building, it may well have a mixture of steel beams and cast-iron columns in it, which seemed to make a happy compromise for builders and designers of the time.

Steel

After iron came the revolution of steel, a mixture of carbon and iron that proved so successful in building that we still use it today. Some steel beams, like RSJs, can only be exposed if their decoration is fireproof. Fireproofing can take the form of painted application as well as the usual boxing in with plasterboard, so if you plan on revealing a steel beam or column in your home, you may need to decorate it with an intumescent paint system.

Fireproofing paints come in two functional types – those that provide fire resistance, and those that restrict surface fire spread. In the case of a beam or column supporting a floor or wall you need the fire-resistance, which means applying a primer and several top coats to build up the finish. This tends to result in a rather thick and textured finish, which is fine if that's what you want, but if you're after a polished, high-gloss look you are going to be disappointed.

Some headway has been made in recent years with water-based, thin-coat systems that are spray-applied, but with care, the finish can be much better. All this means that preparation is all-important and a sand-blasted smooth surface is needed before you start painting. The primer needs to be compatible with the fire-resisting paint and any colour topcoat you might want, and this means using the same manufacturer's recommended products. The obvious advantage of using a thin water-based system is that it reveals the straight edges of the metal and it doesn't give off any nasty VOCs (volatile organic compounds) to breathe in.

Usually only a half-hour period of fire resistance is needed in houses, unless the steel is part of a 'party wall or floor structure', where one hour would be necessary. Since the thickness of any of these materials is governed by the period of fire resistance needed, this keeps the gauge of the covering to a minimum. If you can obtain and apply your chosen product yourself, have a good read of the application conditions; all products have to be applied under a minimum temperature (so cold air is out) and without high humidity (so damp air is out). In some unoccupied rooms you might have to bring in portable radiators to warm and dry out the air. Normally a measuring gauge comes with the product, but you should be aware that some systems are not available for DIY use and must be applied by an authorised system contractor.

Not all metalwork has to be fireproofed, but if it supports walls or floors above, it should be. Roof beams may not require any special treatment at all other than an anti-corrosion primer and architectural paint finish, and very large beams or columns may have inherent fire resistance as a result of being oversized – steel manufacturers list the statistics for all new and historic sections, and part of these are the HP/A ratios that determine fire resistance by size alone.

Joinery
Stripping timber
Old paint should always be removed with proprietary paint strippers that can be brushed on and left overnight to soften the paint before being stripped off. Burning off paint or sanding it off with power sanders are both inadvisable – apart from the fire risk of the first, the latter may mean lead paint particles are released into your home. White lead was once commonly used in paint manufacture and needs some care in the removal. Unwanted timber stains and varnishes are best removed with a solvent-based poultice.

The fashion for stripping timber hasn't stopped at the floorboards, but has carried on up the skirtings and walls to internal doors. Paint, at least for the moment, is not popular on wood; bare wood is definitely in vogue, but I'm not sure for how much

longer, because while softwood pine can look the part in some rural homes, it doesn't look quite so right in urban ones. The Victorians would have painted them right from the start anyway, so stripping them back doesn't hold with authenticity. The exception here is with pre-18th-century oak doors, which were always left undecorated.

For many, removing doors and having them dipped is the quick and easy solution, and indeed it is. But it's not without its troubles – while the stiles and rails of internal doors may be relatively thick, the panels are often anorexically thin and can split in the process. The door you get back may not appear to have the same substance to it as the one you took in. Not only that, but a dip in an acid bath can weaken the glued and tenoned joints, and the two parts of a panel may come apart and need to be glued back together.

Using solvent paint stripper in situ is better for the door, although it will of course take longer to achieve. If you're determined to strip all the doors for that bare-timber look, use beeswax and turpentine to finish them.

Repainting timber
Painting should always begin with a primer and an undercoat, sanded down before the finishing topcoat is applied if a gloss finish is sought. The more time you spend on the preparation for each coat, the better the top finish will be. Masking out around skirtings and architraves is an essential task, and with gloss work it is

always worth using a good-quality brush: picking the bristles out of freshly applied gloss paint is not a good pastime.

MDF (medium-density fibreboard)

You can't write about decorating without mentioning MDF. The smooth face of the board is a joy to paint, and armed with an arsenal of power cutting tools like jigsaws it can be cut easily into any shape you desire – which is why you haven't been able to switch on the TV in the last ten years without seeing it 'transform' somebody's home.

Responsibly, TV companies do make sure that their handymen are wearing masks before the dust flies – and with good reason. When you glue a lot of sawdust together with formaldehyde glue, as makers of MDF have done, you can expect to see its particles go airborne just the same as insulation particles that float forever in the air when you drill and power-cut it. Inhaling them is not good for you, so wearing a fine gauze mask is essential. Some DIY stores will cut your MDF sheet to size for you using a fine power saw with a built-in vacuum sawdust remover. As for the glue used in its manufacture, questions have been raised over formaldehyde and its carcinogenic status. The emissions from the product are thought to be reduced significantly when it is sealed and painted.

I've seen many builders use MDF in new construction to avoid the problems of timber splitting and shrinkage, but some have been surprised by a growth of mould appearing on it later in the damp atmosphere of a freshly plastered room. MDF does not like the damp.

External walls
Brickwork

Saturated brick walls are a problem, even if the dampness isn't getting through to the inside. If the bricks themselves are being soaked and staying that way in winter months, they will more easily be damaged by frost. The combination of rain exposure and frost causes bricks to crack and spall. It's a major pain to have to regularly chop out damaged bricks and replace them, and with older homes it may not be possible to find a suitable match.

It isn't just rain, either: if you live beside a busy road your brickwork may be coated with a film of traffic dirt and the true colour of the bricks may become lost in time. In a Victorian terrace of yellow-stock brick homes, a wall that has been restored by sandblasting will reveal the true golden colour that it was built to, while the others have long since adopted a dark and grimy shade of brown that is gradually turning black; in inner cities, some have turned black. Conservationists are not keen on this process, which radically rejuvenates brick faces.

If you've gone to the trouble of cleaning bricks back to their true colour, you'll be keen for them to stay that way for as long as possible, and treating them with a clear, silicone-based sealant will achieve this. Because they give the wall a sheen that matt brickwork doesn't normally have, you need to try out the product on a few sample bricks or an inconspicuous part of the wall first. They may be fully transparent and clear, but silicone coatings aren't without a certain lustre that you may not be pleased with. Like any paint or coating they have a maintenance life, and the bricks will need to be done again one day – but that could be as much as ten years later. This is a job for a summer day when the wall is thoroughly dry and has been renovated (repointed, cracked bricks replaced, cleaned etc) before you spray or brush on the sealant. Always start at the top of the wall and work down, and try to keep a mental note of what courses you've covered if you stop for tea.

Internal walls and ceilings

Modern emulsions are the easiest of products to apply, as they have just the right consistency to stay on a fully loaded brush or roller and excellent covering abilities. All they really need is a good surface to be applied to, and some masking. Electrical fittings should be removed, with the power switched off at the consumer unit, and pulled forward to allow painting behind them. The same is the case with radiators – although smaller rollers and pads are available for working behind these, only midwives are able use them.

If you've stripped back old wallpaper you might find yourself

against the yellow distemper that preceded modern emulsions. As a finish, it hasn't been brought back into fashion yet. Going back to the Industrial Revolution, soft distempers made from glue and lime-free pigments were popular; they had the earthy tones that we like today, and if your home dates from this era you might appreciate the texture and richness of the colours in this shade. Being water-based, it has no VOCs and also allows the wall to breathe. If you get fed up with it, you can always wash it off – this is one way of identifying it if you think you've found some, as it will come off on a wet finger wiped across it. Lime wash needs a sponge and water and a bit of elbow grease to be removed, but soft distemper isn't that durable. It should be applied with the largest flat brush you can get your hands on, and you'll need to work fast, because it dries rapidly.

Coving

There are plasterers and decorators who specialise in fixing coving, and others who specialise in avoiding it. It's one job that looks simple but can be painfully difficult to get right. To begin with, the depth choice has to suit the room and its style of décor, but that's the easy bit. Cutting the corner mitres is where the fun starts, and although the makers of plaster coving are kind enough to provide paper templates with them, the corners of rooms can be a long way from square and helpful.

Fixing coving is often done with alternatives to purpose-made adhesives which go off quickly. Textured plastic paint (Artex) mixed to a stiff consistency is sometimes used to create a long-lasting adhesive that can give you more time to get it in position. Nails are used to underpin in situ, and some filling of joints is always necessary to create that perfect transition between wall and ceiling, providing of course you paint it white. This might not be the last labour, but coving draws a smooth line around your home and finishes it off beautifully, and so it seems an appropriate conclusion to this handbook.

Time to relax!

Glossary

Bakelite
An early plastic invented in 1916

Bressummer
A long beam over a fireplace

BTU
British thermal unit

Close-boarded roof
Where the rafters are clad on the tile side with timber boarding

Coping
Weathering stone or course to the top of a wall

Corbelling
Successive courses of projecting brickwork

De-rating
Allowing for insulation overheating in electric cables

Dentil course
A projecting course of stone or brick

Fenestration
Architecture of windows

Finial
A pointed ornament to a gable end

Flashing
Weathering between a roof covering and wall/chimney

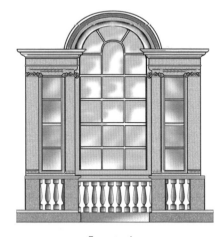

Fenestration

Flemish bond
A 17th-century brick bond of alternate headers and stretchers in each course

Fletton
A type of cheap brick

Header
The end face of a brick

Horn
A projection on the cill of a window or door frame to help build it in to a wall

Lath-and-plaster
Plaster laid over thin split strips of wood

Loop-in circuits
Lighting circuit that reduces T-joints using ceiling roses

Low-e glass
Low-emissivity (reflective) coated double glazing

No fines concrete
Concrete made without sand

Ogee
Architectural moulding shape used for mouldings and architraves.

Optimum start control
Boiler ignition control used to reach programmed room temperatures within a given time

Parapet
A low wall to the edge of a roof, balcony or gutter

Quoin
A brick or stone set in the corner of a wall

Radial circuits
A spur circuit leading off a ring circuit without looping back

Ridge
The apex of a roof

Snap header
A half-brick (not a header)

Solvent-weld plumbing
Glued permanent joints of plastic pipe

Stucco
Smooth external plastering

Spalling
Frost damage to bricks

Soakers
Undertile weatherings

Stretcher
The long face of a brick

Terrazzo
Coloured floor stone mosaic

Tusk tenon
A small tenon joint

Voussoir
A wedge-shaped arch brick

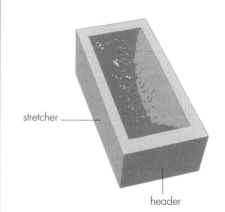

stretcher

header

Brick

Useful Contacts

Association of Building Engineers (ABE)
01604 404121
www.abe.org.uk

British Interior Design Association
020 7349 0800
www.bida.org.uk

British Wood Preserving and Damp-proofing Association
01332 225100
www.bwpda.co.ul

British Standards Institute
020 8996 9000
www.bsi.org.uk

The Building Centre
020 7692 4000
www.buildingcentre.co.uk

The Building Conservation Directory
01747 871717
www.buildingconservation.co.uk

Building Research Establishment (BRE)
01923 664 4000
www.bre.co.uk

BRE Scotland
01355 576200
www.bre.co.uk

Cadw: Welsh Historic Monuments
02920 500200
www.cadw.wales.gov.uk

Council for Registered Gas Installers (CORGI)
01256 372200
www.corgi-gas.com

English Heritage
0870 333 1181
www.english-heritage.org.uk

Environment and Heritage Service Northern Ireland
028 9054 3034
www.ehsni.gov.uk

Federation of Master Builders
020 7242 7583
www.fmb.org

The Georgian Group
020 7529 8920
www.georgiangroup.org.uk

Heritage Building Contractors Group
01543 414234
www.buildingconservation.com

Historic Scotland
0131 668 8600
www.historic-scotland.gov.uk

**Institute of Historic Building
Conservation**
01747 871717
www.ihbc.co.uk

Institute of Plumbing
01708 472791
www.plumbers.org.uk

**Kitchen Bathroom Bedroom
Specialists Association**
01905 621787
www.ksa.co.uk

National Federation of Builders
020 7608 5000
www.theCC.org.uk

National Fireplace Association
0121 200 1310
www.nationalfireplaceassociation.org.
uk

**National Inspection Council for
Electrical Installation Contracting
(NICEIC)**
020 7564 2323
www.niceic.org.uk

Plastic Window Federation
01582 456147
www.pwfed.co.uk

**Royal Incorporation of Architects
in Scotland (RIAS)**
0131 229 7545
www.rias.org.uk

**Royal Institution of British
Architects (RIBA)**
020 7580 5533
www.riba.org

**Royal Institution of Chartered
Surveyors (RICS)**
020 7222 7000
www.rics.org.uk

**Scottish Society for Conservation
and Restoration (SSCR)**
01506 811777
www.sscr.demon.co.uk

**The Society for the Protection of
Ancient Buildings (SPAB)**
020 7377 1644
www.spab.org.uk

Solid Fuel Association
0845 601 4406
www.solidfuel.co.uk

Twentieth Century Society
020 7250 3857
www.c20society.demon.co.uk

Victorian Society
020 8994 1019
www.victorian-society.org.uk

Index